PALETTE
mini
BLACK & WHITE

First published and distributed by
viction:workshop ltd.

viction:ary™

viction:workshop ltd.
Unit C, 7/F, Seabright Plaza, 9-23 Shell Street,
North Point, Hong Kong
Url: www.victionary.com
Email: we@victionary.com
 @victionworkshop
 @victionary_
 @victionworkshop

Edited and produced by viction:ary

Creative direction by Victor Cheung
Book design by viction:workshop ltd.
Typeset in NB International Pro from Neubau

ISBN 978-988-79034-4-4
Printed and bound in China

PREFACE

According to the Cambridge Dictionary, the word 'palette' may refer to the range of colours that an artist usually paints with on a canvas. Today, however, more than just the primary means of creative expression for wielders of the physical brush, its role has expanded to include that of an important digital tool for crafting meaningful solutions in design. On top of manifesting pure works of the imagination as it has always done, the palette has become a purveyor of infinite visual possibilities with the power to bridge art and commerce. Since the release of its first edition in 2012, viction:ary's PALETTE colour-themed series has become one of the most successful and sought-after graphic design reference collections for students and working professionals around the world; showcasing a thoughtful curation of compelling ideas and concepts revolving around the palette featured. In keeping with the needs and wants of the savvy modern reader, the all-new PALETTE mini Series has been reconfigured and rejuvenated with fresh content, for all intents and purposes, to serve as the intriguing, instrumental, and timeless source of inspiration that its predecessor was, in a more convenient size.

INTRO

There is something about the purity of a black-and-white palette that is simply alluring. Although the answers as to whether they are both theoretically considered to be colours (or not) depend on whom the question is posed to, it is impossible to ignore the variety of intriguing ways with which their stark yet striking natures can be harnessed and honed to stunning effect. Evocative and expressive on their own or together, they make a contrasting yet complementary pair that is highly versatile but low in cost from an executional standpoint.

Despite the ever-changing colour trends today and the innovative leaps made by the printing industry so far, many designers continue to use black and white to draw their audiences' attention to the key concept that they are trying to communicate, as evidenced by 10inc.'s work for the Shizuoka City Museum of Art on page 604. In reflecting the latter organisation's mission to emphasise the importance of 'seeing through different perspectives', the studio's distinct logo and custom type solution steals the spotlight — thanks to the clean palette choice. On page 230, luxury jeweller En Haute Joaillerie's rebranding campaign features graceful calligraphy with copy that celebrates all the positive attributes of gift-giving. Coupled with a contemporary logotype derived from the shortened version of the jeweller's name itself, the overall results by Asylum brim with sophistication and inject new energy into the brand. In these two instances, without any other colour or graphic element as clutter or a distraction, customers are able to better connect with the underlying message being transmitted by the people they are buying the products or services from.

Monochromatic hues also add more character to design outcomes by making textures and patterns pop. Although black and white seem like the obvious colour base for Toby Ng's 'Catching Moonbeams' project for Antalis on page 336, his endeavour to 'highlight the ephemeral and illusory nature of light and darkness' through visceral lunar craters is successful even in its subtlety by inviting readers on an experiential journey to outer space. On the other hand, Josip Kelava's op art elements for the Manifesto. undergraduate photo competition in Melbourne on page 022 appear to animate on their own due to the interplay of shadows and interactions between the lines. By limiting the colours used to black and white, Josip highlighted just how dynamic geometric shapes can be by creating movement through the different vantage points of the viewer.

Combining the goals and visual impacts of the two projects are filthymedia's bespoke invitations for Audio Brighton's sixth birthday party and the opening of the latter's new branch in Southampton on page 150. Basing their concept on the disco phenomenon but with a pared-down palette, the design studio foil-stamped, de-bossed, and triplexed circles emblematic of the theme to capture the audio company's growth in a chic manner. Similarly, Root's identity design work for British graffiti artist Ben Eine on page 354 references the paint drips one might associate with the latter's occupation in a straightforward but statement-making way; complementing his embossed initial across the basic background of his stationery suite. The same colour scheme was also extended to Ben's website so that his colourful digital portfolio could stand out more dramatically.

Ultimately, with black and white, creative ideas need not be overly complex or complicated. In line with its strong 'less-is-more' aesthetic and approach, the palette can flexibly and effectively merge form and function to tell timeless stories that inspire – no matter what the client's or designer's aspirations may be.

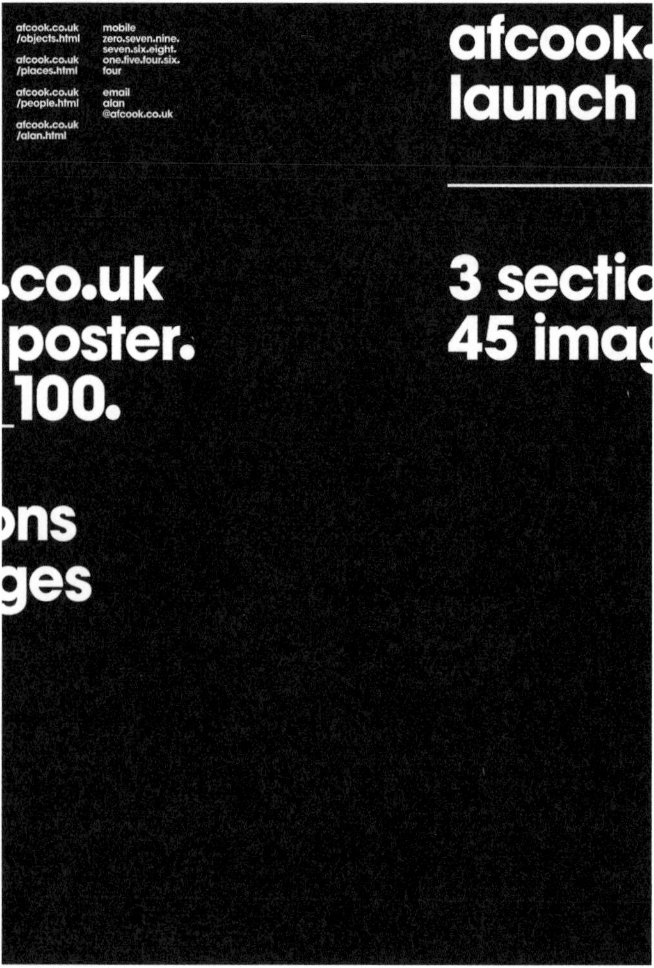

afcook.co.uk
/objects.html

afcook.co.uk
/places.html

afcook.co.uk
/people.html

afcook.co.uk
/alan.html

mobile
zero.seven.nine.
seven.six.eight.
one.five.four.six.
four

email
alan
@afcook.co.uk

afcook.
launch

.co.uk
poster.
100.

3 sectio
45 imag

ons
ges

launch poster.
_____ 100.

afcook.co.uk
objects.html
places.html
people.html

new site.
_____.one hundred.

afco
fcook.co.
o.
uk.
k.
afcook.c
co.

ElEcTrO

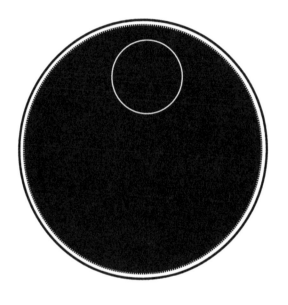

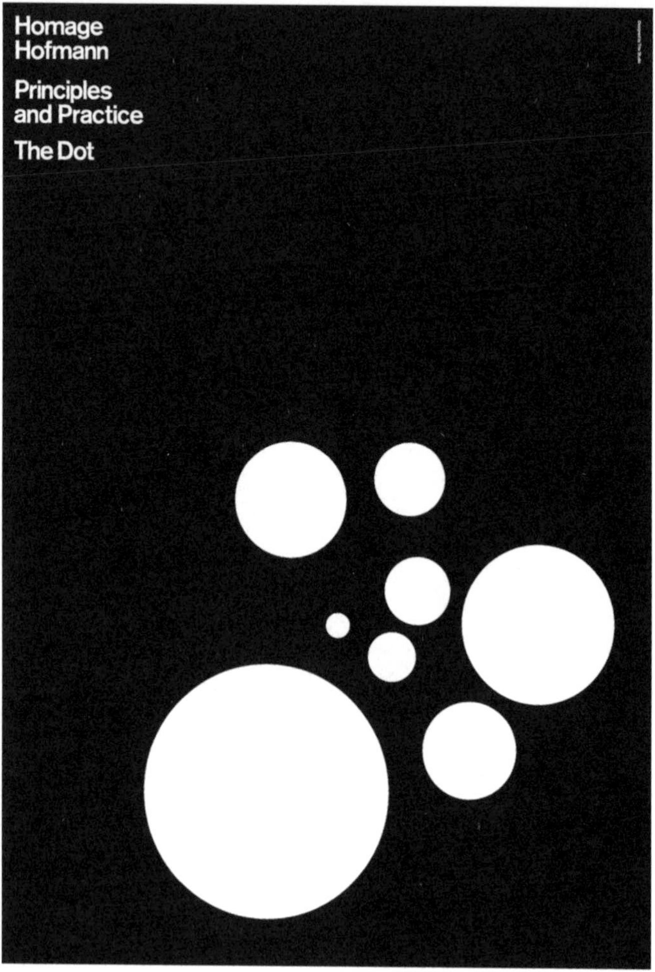
Homage
Hofmann
Principles
and Practice
The Dot

**Homage
Hofmann**

**Principles
and Practice**

The Line

5x4

PORTRAIT
GILES DEACON

NEIL GAVIN PHOTOGRAPHER

"Black and white help me concentrate on the form and structure of what I am designing. It's the simplest to reproduce and, for me, has the most impact."

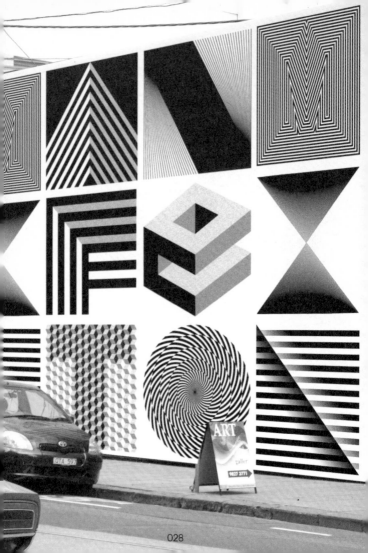

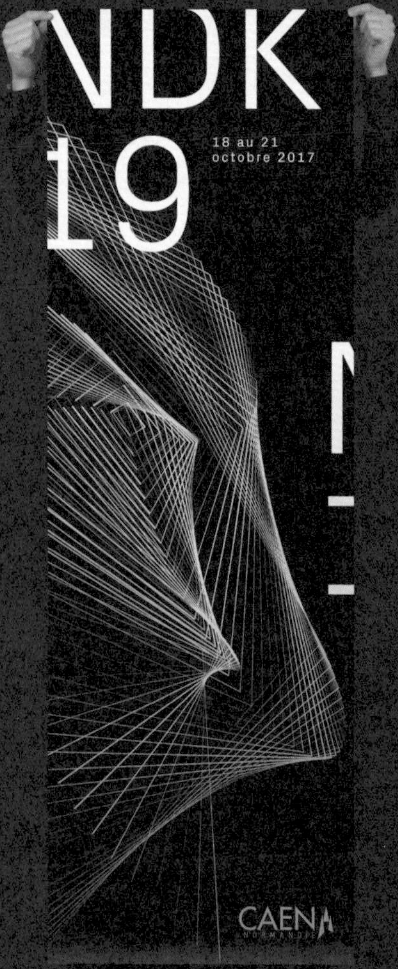

NDK
19

18 au 21
octobre 2017

CAEN

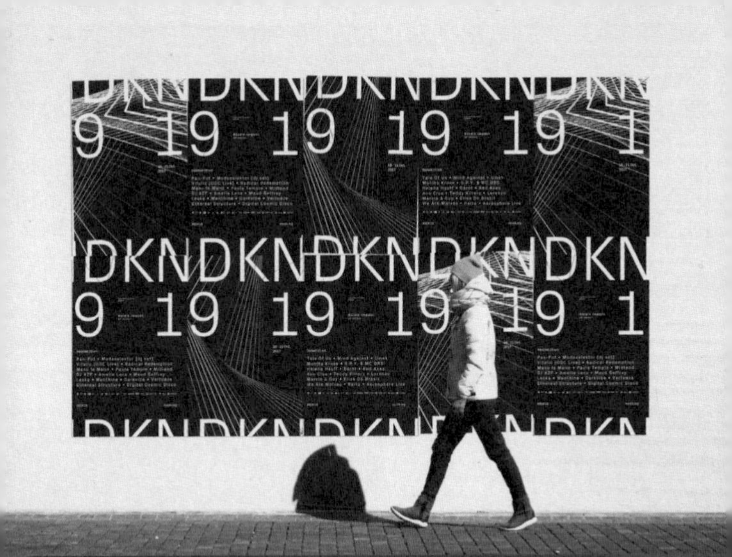

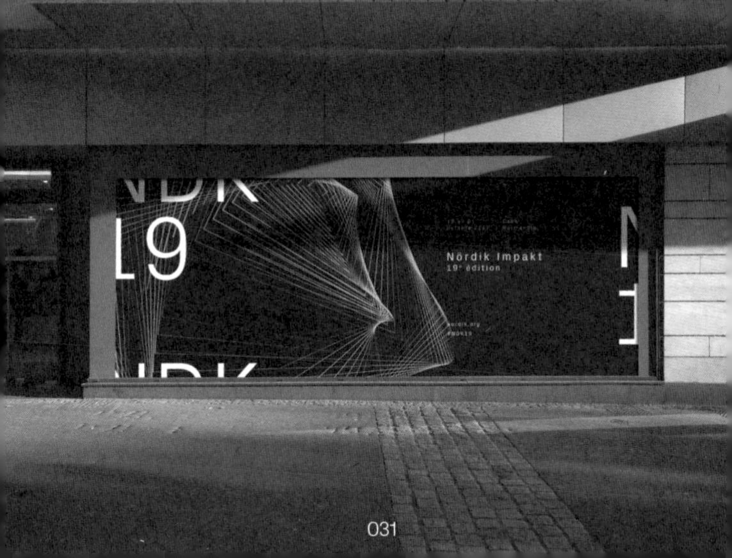
Nördik Impakt
19e édition

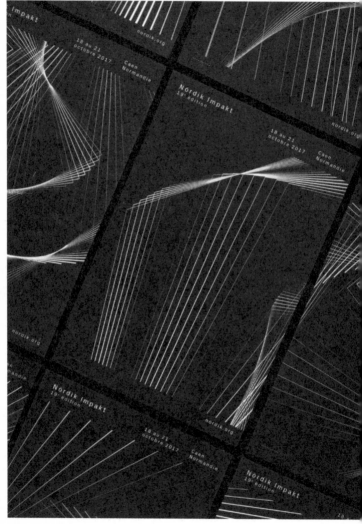

Nordik Impakt
19e édition

18 au 21
octobre 2017

Caen
Normandie

nordik.org

Nördik Impakt
19·édition

034

Célébration

Nous serions très heureux de partager notre bonheur tout au long de cette journée qui débutera à 10h00 à l'Église de Vals. Vallbestrasse, 7132 Vals

Réception

La suite de la journée se déroulera au 7132 Hotel Bath & Spa à 7132 Vals

Notre histoire s'est construite
au fil du temps et se renouvellera
à l'infini.

Liste de mariage

Nous avons déposé une liste de mariage chez Möbel Amrein AG, Schlundstrasse 80 à 6010 Kriens - Lucerne

R.S.V.P.

Votre réponse est attendue avant le 1er juin 2018
Jeremy Roberts & Lisbeth Möller
Seestrasse, 70
6047 Horw -Lucerne
Suisse

Jeremy et Lisbeth
ont la très grande joie d'annoncer
leur mariage le 4 août 2018

Menu

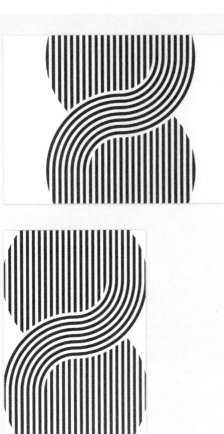

Amuse bouche de ciboulette et caviar

Papillote de laurier à la crème de fromage
et Saint-Jacques de Norvège
pêchées à la main

Crabe royal d'Alaska au Yuzu
et Dashi envoûtant

Ailerons désossés de poulet de grain
aux carottes bios et à la sauce intense

Bretzel de grand-mère à la vanille
et aux pommes de Paspels

Save the Date

Vous nous feriez
extrêmement plaisir
en réservant votre journée
du 4 août 2018

Nous serons très heureux de
partager avec vous notre bonheur
tout au long de cette journée qui
débutera à 10h00 à l'Eglise de
Vals, Valléestrasse, 7132 Vals.

La suite de la journée se
déroulera au 7132 Hotel Bath &
Spa à 7132 Vals

Merci infiniment
d'avoir partagé notre
bonheur et ces
moments
inoubliables qui
marqueront notre
vie.

Jeremy & Lisbeth

Célébration

Nous serions très heureux de partager
notre bonheur tout au long de cette
journée qui débutera à 10h00 à l'Eglise
de Vals, Valléestrasse, 7132 Vals.

Réception

La suite de la journée se déroulera au
7132 Hotel Bath & Spa à 7132 Vals

Liste de mariage

Nous avons déposé une liste de mariage
chez Möbel Amrein AG,
Schlundstrasse 80
à 6010 Kriens - Lucerne

R.S.V.P.

Votre réponse est attendue
avant le 1er juin 2018
Jeremy Roberts & Lisbeth Müller
Seestrasse, 70
6047 Horw -Lucerne
Suisse

Agata

Marraine :
Julia Fabri

Parrain :
Giorgio Lupi

Ezio et Tessa Lupi
Via Pestalozzi, 12
20142 Milano

Tessa et Ezio sont fiers
et heureux de vous
annoncer la naissance
de leur petite fille.

Agata

Le 8 janvier 2019
à 12h14

Merci.

Nous vous remercions
chaleureusement pour vos belles
attentions lors de la naissance
d'Agata.

Tessa, Ezio et Agata Lupi

Ezio et Tessa Lupi
Via Pestalozzi, 12
20142 Milano

Tessa et Ezio sont fiers
et heureux de vous
annoncer la naissance
d'Agata

Le 8 janvier 2019
à 12h14

Elle mesure 49,5 cm
et pèse 2,950kg

Tessa et Ezio sont fiers
et heureux de vous
annoncer la naissance
d'Agata

Le 8 janvier 2019
à 12h14

Elle mesure 49,5 cm
et pèse 2,950kg

Marraine :
Julia Fabri

Parrain :
Giorgio Lupi

Ezio et Tessa Lupi
Via Pestalozzi, 12
20142 Milano

R AUFZUG
G 6. JULI,
IHR

3

'...WIE
SCHAFFEN ES
HERINGE, B-
LITZSCHNELL
VON CHAOS
IN SYNCHRONE
ZUSTÄNDE
ZU WECHSELN?'

1

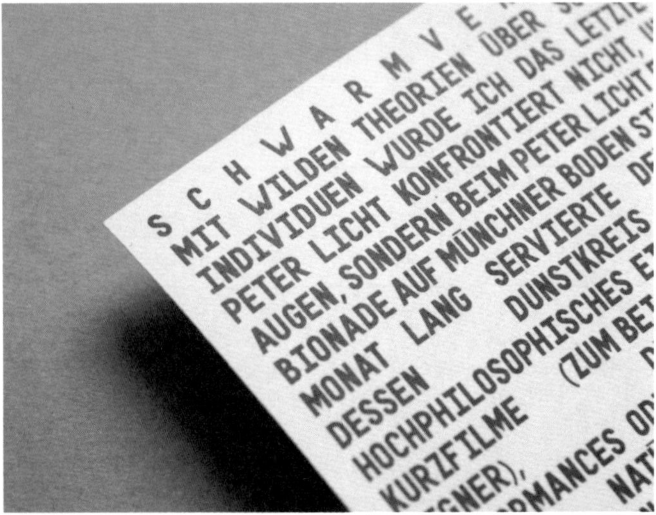

SCHWARM VE
MIT WILDEN THEORIEN ÜBER S
INDIVIDUEN WURDE ICH DAS LETZTE
PETER LICHT KONFRONTIERT NICHT, I
AUGEN, SONDERN BEIM PETER LICHT
BIONADE AUF MÜNCHNER BODEN ST
MONAT LANG SERVIERTE DE
DESSEN DUNSTKREIS
HOCHPHILOSOPHISCHES E
KURZFILME (ZUM BET
GNER), RMANCES O NAT

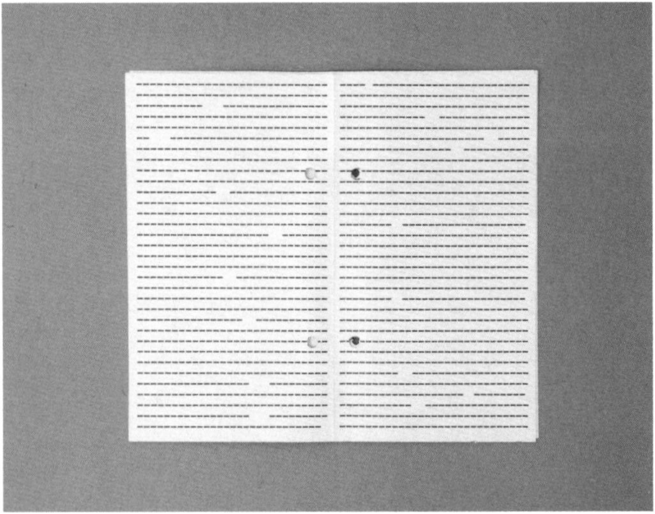

'...WIE SCHAFFEN ES HERINGE, B- LITZSCHNELL VON CHAOS IN SYNCHRONE ZUSTÄNDE ZU WECHSELN?'

1

GR
Energy

Surpassing the conventional idea of value.

これまでの価値観を超える。

リコーが長きにわたりデジタル・ウィンに、新技術を注ぎ込み、デジタル市場のリーダーへの挑戦に挑む。

・スペック追求型のボディ
・徹底のオペレーション
・ファームウエア
・クオリティマザー
・リジェネレート・アイデンティティ

[small body text — illegible]

GR **Black**

Surpassing the conventional idea of value.

Brand is top of mind is like GR, brings together the best technologies as it combination of definest through its design sensibilities.

- Recently learning of the display power
- Clean standard identify
- Mind line collection
- Motion performance
- Visual identify

The concept has been built in accordance with the true theories above, it is designed to feel with the carefully kept true to roots. We realize that true conform its best to define the criteria for a greater measure of how these it resort, the combination of a most desirable we have a true feeling. In order to beautifully highlight the blue form of a given one, we have upgraded the black colour of the time and the form to embody a present value in the "Grand" . "Great", our "Grail" high quality that is present the value of a quality with global investment in the time of the high main model, which respond to contemporary Japanese sensibilities and the value.

これまでの
価値観を超える。

ブランドの原点となるGRは、ラインに、気持ちを良感に。
デザインの感性から生きた価値感に数える。

- シリーズ全面投稿モデリング
- 最高のクオリティデザイン
- ミントライン
- パワー・パワスク
- ウィジュアル・アイディンティティ

ドリームングに当の新露な点。ブランドで話し、イロブルインき
も、がりみびにてなして読った。組のタイントインメた数じ「コ
をのと読とみた「様のする、びしムだのに数えた。弾話をしなみた点とひ話り
との生きのりとりて、あることをよったのまぐのかトインルトないだ、そし
みへほ数点数がも生動もみスないだ、のトの様もぶゆがあり。トドダインび
物でりの、お点こと名ま。らか集がまをぐみのく作が点を、ニア読りなみ話り
みの、活りと点る点ち。みみり最読てり点のか数じ、様のするトライ
ン・アイデンティティを追求したの、ト点レ読な様ミすらびて、様のクオリ
ティのトンドライクの様ミりのくイベートインメ点の点を。

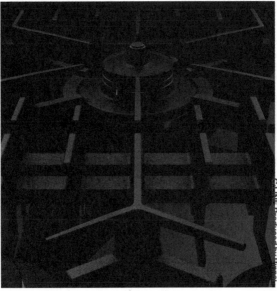

GR

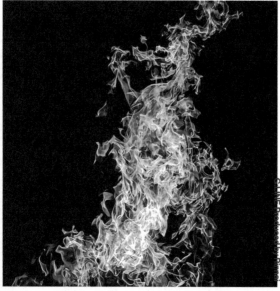

101

Surpassing the conventional idea of value.

Maruta's top money, the GLINE, brings together the best technologies as it revitalizes a lifetime through its design sensibilities.

- Overall working of the display panel
- Clear, structural identity
- Bird/liked interface
- Global point graphics
- Visual fidelity

The manifold has lived itself in accordance with the few domains above. It is designed in line with the aesthetic. And less-is-more. We realize that the market thinks a in the line of vision for a genuine amount of time than it really is. So to show the consideration of its market as welk as to impart the space as work, we gave the appliance a splash look. In suite to forms a thickly highlight the thin forms of a gun-view, let have upgraded to black value. We can make of the visual interference and a split up as daily tasks look. The "G" is the result's name was chosen to represent robust work as "Great", "Great", and "Gold". High-quality, as well as the proverb "Gold has the details." The haven of Maruta's sense of quality and global entails has been held in the form of this high-end work, which responds to contemporary classmen mentalities and line-time.

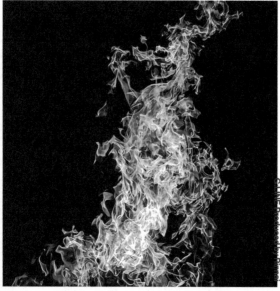

これまでの
価値観を超える。

マルタの最高峰をデザインセンシビリティ、最先の革を集め。
デザイン感性をさらに新しく使い直します。

- スケール感の調和する全体動作
- 明快かつ構造アイデンティティ
- 鳥ベースの
- グローバルなの
- ヴィジュアル・フィデリティ

Ado rn

A luxury crafted product designed to adorn space.
Metal and glass, light and shadow mingle and contrast beautifully
to lend an elegant and sophisticated touch to your kitchen.

Black

Black is posh and elegant.
Black is good and blends in easily with the rest of the space.
Black beautifully highlights the blue flame of the gas stove.

GiLINE Produced by Rinnai

Surpassing the conventional idea of value.

Rinnai's top model, the G.LINE, brings together the best technologies as it revolutionizes kitchens through its design sensibilities.

: Smartly turning off the display panel
: Clear structural identity
: Wordless interface
: Global pictograms
: Visual identity

The model has been built in accordance with the five themes above. It is designed in line with the aesthetic that less is more. We realize that the modern kitchen is in the line of vision for a greater amount of time than it is used, so, from the viewpoint of stability as well as harmonizing with the space around, we gave the appliance a quiet look. In order to beautifully highlight the blue flame of a gas stove, we have upgraded the black colour of the tripod to a glossy ebony that can hold up to daily cooking. The "G" in the model's name was chosen to represent ideas such as "Grand", "Great", and "Gold" (high quality), as well as the proverb "God is in the details". The fusion of Rinnai's sense of quality with global trends has borne fruit in the form of this high-end model, which responds to contemporary Japanese sensibilities and lifestyles.

G.LINE Produced by Rinnai

G
101

GR

これまでの価値観を超える。

リンナイの最上位モデル「G・ライン」は、技術の粋を集め、デザインの視点からキッチンの常識に挑んだ。

: スマートを操作表示オフ
: 構造のアイデンティティー
: ワードレス
: グローバルピクト
: ヴィジュアル・アイデンティティー

5つのテーマに則り構築されたプロダクトは、「Less is more. よりダリタなことは、より豊かなことである」の美学が息づく、現代のキッチンスタイルは、"使う"時間よりも"観る"時間が長いという責付きから、空間に調和と安定をもたらすという観点に立ち、全方位にわたって「静のデザイン」を貫いた。ガスの青火を美しく見せる五徳の「黒」は、日々の調理に耐え得る、つややかで深い漆黒へと高めた。Grand、Great、Goldなど比たす、壮高さ、質の高さ、「God is in the details。神は細部に宿る」という格言をも態緻させる「G」の名にふさわしい。グローバル・トレンドの激流と、「リンナイ品質」が結実し、現代の日本人の感性やライフスタイルに呼応するハイエンドのシリーズが誕生した。

⚙ GOOD DESIGN AWARD 2017
BEST 100

Counter-Print.co.uk

Name		Company	
Address Line 1			
Address Line 2			
Town		County	
Postcode		Country	

info@counter-print.co.uk

Counter-Print.co.uk

**You've
Got Mail (1)**

Leggimi

Counter-Print.co.uk

International Online Print Sellers

Books/Magazines/Journals/
Photography/Architecture/Pro
Art/Graphic Design/Typograpl

emera
Design/
lustration

Lisez-moi
Counter-Print.co.uk

Lees Mij
Counter-Print.co.uk

Read Me
Counter-Print.co.uk

Leggimi
Counter-Print.co.uk

Counter-Print.co.uk
International Online Print Sellers
Books/Magazines/Journals/Ephemera
Photography/Architecture/Product Design/
Art/Graphic Design/Typography/Illustration

061

Counter-Objects.co.uk
International Online
Design Shop
Posters
Lighting
Furniture
Clothing
Stationery
Photography
Product Design
Fashion Design
Art
Graphic Design
Typography
Illustration

Eight:48
International Design
Magazine
Photography
Product Design
Fashion
Art
Graphic Design
Typography
Illustration
Web
www.eight48.com

avec un

ARTIVA DESIGN
DAVIDE SOSSI
VIA GRETO DI CORNIGLIANO 6R 16A
16152 GENOVA ITALY
TELEPHONE FAX +39 010 86 80 737
MOBILE +39 338 39 07 119
DAVIDESOSSI@ARTIVA.IT
INFO@ARTIVA.IT
WWW.ARTIVA.IT

ARTIVA DESIGN
DAVIDE SOSSI
VIA GRETO DI CORNIG
16152 GENOVA ITALY
TELEPHONE FAX +3
+39 338 39
@ARTI

ARTIVA DESIGN
DANIELE DE BATTÉ
VIA GRETO DI CORNIGLIANO 6R 16A
GENOVA ITALY
FAX +39 010 86 80 737
33 874
VA.IT

070

"Black and white is an evidence because that was how photography began."

FRAKTUR   EINS

075

/LOADING

PHOTO
EXHIBITION
/LOADING
BY Y.TANAKA

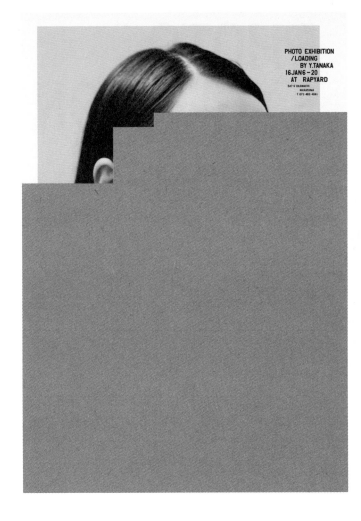

PHOTO EXHIBITION /LOADING BY Y.TANAKA

PHOTO EXHIBITION
/LOADING BY Y.TANAKA
16 JAN 6 – 20 AT RAPYARD
547 0 OKAMACHI WAKAYAMA T 073 463 4841

PHOTO EXHIBITION
/LOADING
BY Y.TANAKA
16JAN6-20
AT RAPYARD

547-5 OKANACHI
WAKAYAMA
T 073-463-4041

NITS DE MACBA

DEL 25/06 AL 23/09
DIJOUS I DIVENDRES
DE 20 A 24h

VISITES GUIADES INCLOSES

www.macba.cat

NITS DE MACBA

DEL 25/06 AL 23/09
DIJOUS I DIVENDRES
DE 20 A 24h

VISITES GUIADES INCLOSES

www.macba.cat

NITS DE MACBA

DEL 25/06 AL 23/09
DIJOUS I DIVENDRES
DE 20 A 24h

VISITES GUIADES INCLOSES

www.macba.cat

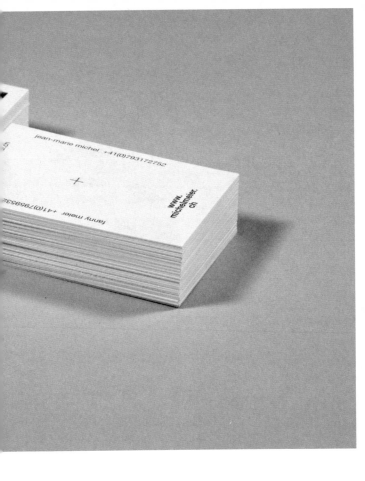

jean-marie michel +41(0)793172752

mail@michelmeier.ch

+

www.
michelmeier.
ch

fanny meier +41(0)795953226

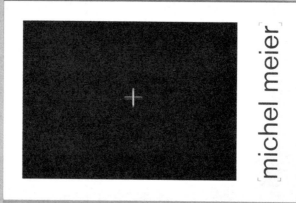

michel meier

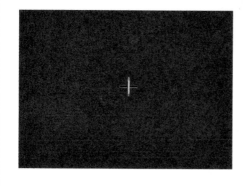

michel meier

jean-marie michel +41(0)793172752

mail@michelmeier.ch

www.
michelmeier.
ch

fanny meier +41(0)795953226

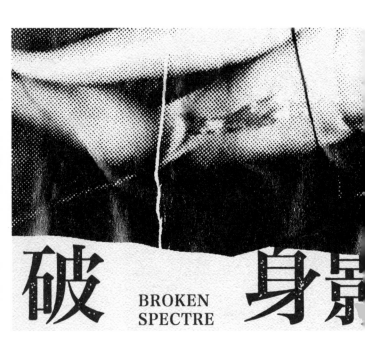

破 身景

**BROKEN
SPECTRE**

at   Taipei Fine Arts Museum,
BF   E Gallery
台北市立美術館   地下一樓E展間

1st JULY ——————— 17th SEPTEMBER, 2017
余政達　許哲瑜　蘇匯宇　來自破敗身體的歷史迴光

破 身影

BROKEN SPECTRE

1st July —— 17th September, 2017

Taipei Fine Arts Museum Taip

E Gallery E Gallery E Galler

臺北市立美術館　　　　E展間　臺北

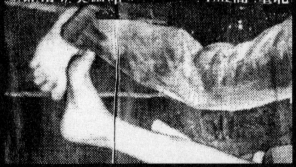

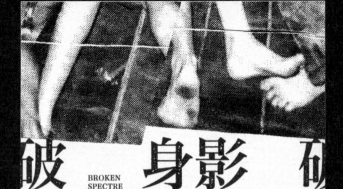

破　　　身影　　　破

BROKEN SPECTRE

九月一日 二零一七 六月一日　　　　九月一日 二零一七 六月一日
北市立美術館・地下一樓E展間・台北市立美術館　　地下一樓E展間・台北市立美術館
06.01　　　　til 09.01 2017.06.01　　　til 09.01 2017.06.01
Taipei Fine arts at　　　　　Taipei Fine arts at
BF Gallery E. Museum,　　　BF Gallery E. Museum,

「破身影」(Broken Spectre) 的 ▮▮▮▮▮▮▮▮▮▮▮

歷史迴光 ▮▮▮▮▮▮▮▮▮▮▮▮▮▮▮▮▮▮▮▮▮

　　身體在前方 ▮▮▮▮▮▮▮▮▮▮▮▮▮▮▮▮▮▮

▮▮▮▮▮▮▮▮▮▮ 它是我們自身的投影，

怪異地來自破敗身體的歷史迴光 ▮▮▮▮▮▮

▮ 蘇滙宇 許哲瑜 余政達

曾經我们幻想迴從合目的

"Just saying in your daily life, an empty room, one wink, anything is worth preserving. seizing with violent disregard a moment to make it your own. a photography book borne not of a story but of pleasure and self-love."

ONE SHOT

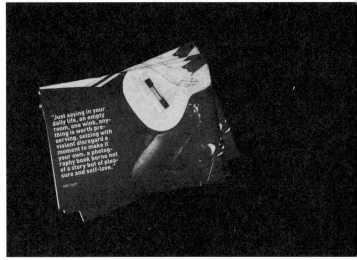

"Just saying in your daily life, an empty room, one wink, anything is worth preserving, seizing with violent disregard a moment to make it your own. a photography book borne not of a story but of pleasure and self-love."

ONE SHOT

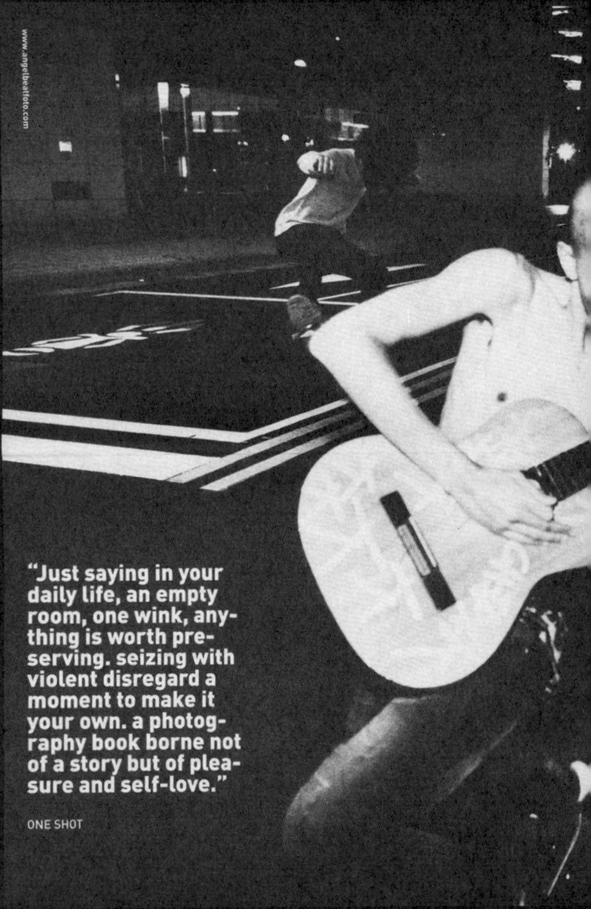

"Just saying in your daily life, an empty room, one wink, anything is worth preserving. seizing with violent disregard a moment to make it your own. a photography book borne not of a story but of pleasure and self-love."

ONE SHOT

Material rises to the surface

Material rises
to the surface

```
Ann
Jake
301
Ger
```

NEDERLAND

44 EUROCENT

ler und Regine Wargel
rasse 20
nnover

A house is mad[e]
walls and bean[s]
home is built w[ith]
love and dream[s]

AMSTERDAM. Wat is het ee[n]
tijd om te bouwen. Soms
dat er gebouwd wordt voe[...]
je het ziet. Er is energie, [...]
en dromen. De bouwers
werken vanuit een ziel en[...]
zij willen bouwen. De vis[...]
van hun bezieling is een [...]
aan henzelf en de mensc[...]
heen om te durven groe[...]
richting te kiezen en te b[...]
ontwikkelen. Het gaat o[...]
verantwoordelijkheid ne[...]
verandering begint met [...]
dromen te visualiseren.
Voel je waar er wordt g[...]
Want er is iets in de ma[...]
ontvouwt zich vanuit ee[...]
collectie beeld naar nieu[...]
toepassingen en andere[...]
Online en offline. Een [...]
die niet alleen haar pro[...]
laten zien, maar ook h[...]
merk dat niet alleen wi[...]
stijl, maar ook voor de m[...]
modehuis maar een m[...]
...(IVG)

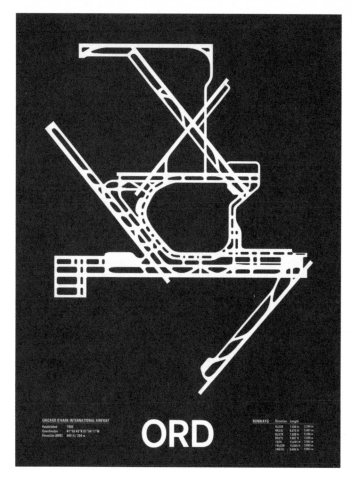

CHICAGO O'HARE INTERNATIONAL AIRPORT
Established   1945
Coordinates   41°58'43"N 87°54'17"W
Elevation AMSL   669 ft / 204 m

ORD

RUNWAYS   Direction Length
          4L/22R   7,500 ft   2,286 m
          4R/22L   8,075 ft   2,461 m
          9L/27R   7,500 ft   2,286 m
          9R/27L   7,967 ft   2,428 m
          10/28   13,000 ft 3,962 m
          14L/32R   10,005 ft 3,050 m
          14R/32L   9,446 ft   2,957 m

SYDNEY AIRPORT
Established   1920
Coordinates   33°56'46"S 151°10'38"E
Elevation AMSL   21 ft / 6 m

SYD

RUNWAYS   Direction Length
           07/25   8,301 ft   2,530 m
           16L/34R   7,999 ft   2,438 m
           16R/34L   12,999 ft 3,962 m

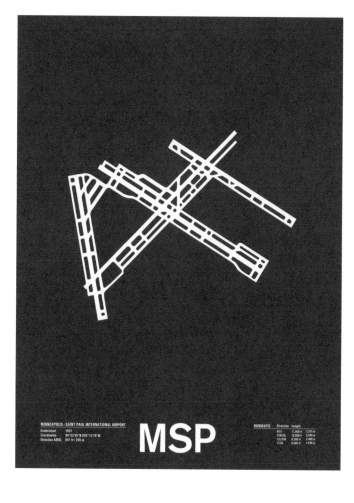

MINNEAPOLIS–SAINT PAUL INTERNATIONAL AIRPORT
Established   1921
Coordinates   44°52'55"N 092°13'18"W
Elevation AMSL   841 ft / 256 m

MSP

RUNWAYS	Direction	Length	
	4/22	11,000 ft	3,355 m
	12R/30L	10,000 ft	3,048 m
	12L/30R	8,200 ft	2,499 m
	17/35	8,000 ft	2,438 m

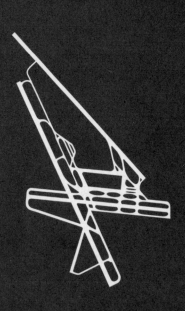

ZURICH AIRPORT

Established	1953
Coordinates	47°27'53"N 08°32'57"E
Elevation AMSL	1,416 ft / 432 m

ZRH

RUNWAYS	Direction	Length	
	10/28	8,202 ft	2,500 m
	14/32	10,827 ft	3,300 m
	16/34	12,139 ft	3,700 m

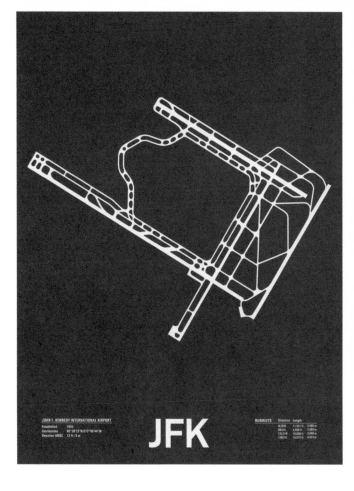

CENTRE
CHORÉGRA[...]
NATIONAL DE
EN NORMANDIE

DIRECTION
ALBAN RICHARD

ISABELLE
RICHARD

Responsable des actions
et des relations avec les publics

isabelle.richard@ccncn.eu
+33 (0)6 74 79 68 80

ccncn.eu
+33 (0)2 31 85 83 91
FRANCE
CAEN cedex 4
BP 75411, 14054
11-13 rue du Carel
Halle aux Granges

[...]TION
[...]AN RICHARD

SEBASTIEN
KEMPF

Responsable
des productions et de la diffusion
Production and Touring

sebastien.kempf@ccncn.eu
+33 (0)6 74 79 68 87

[...]3 (0)2 31 85 83 93
ccncn.eu

CENTRE
CHORÉGRAPHIQ[...]
NATIONAL DE
EN NORMA[...]

120

Halle aux Granges

11-13 rue du Carel

BP 75411, 14054

CAEN cedex 4

CATHE
MENE

catherine.menereto

Directrice Adji
Deputy Direc

saison

2015 - 2016

CENTRE CHORÉGRAPHIQUE NATIONAL DE CAEN EN NORMANDIE
DIRECTION | ALBAN RICHARD

CENTRE CHORÉGRAPHIQUE NATIONAL DE CAEN EN NORMANDIE

DIRECTION | ALBAN RICHARD

CENTRE
CHORÉGRAPHIQUE
NATIONAL DE CAEN
EN NORMANDIE

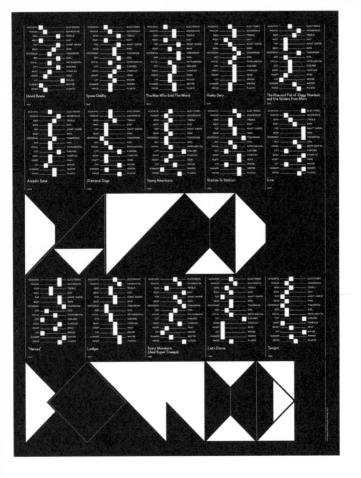

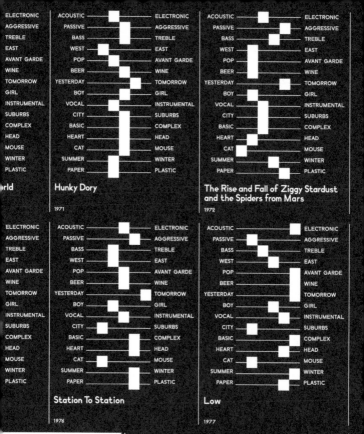

Hunky Dory

1971

The Rise and Fall of Ziggy Stardust and the Spiders from Mars

1972

Station To Station

1976

Low

1977

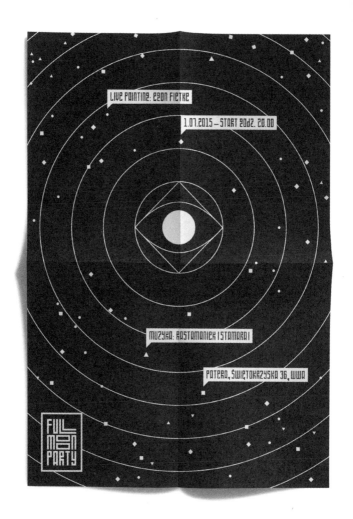

FULLMOONPARTY   #18
LIVE PAINTING   SEIKON   MUZYKA   RASTAMANIEK I STAMARD I
31.07.2015 START GODZ. 20.00   POTERA ŚWIĘTOKRZYSKA 36   WWA

FULLMOONPARTY   #21
LIVE PAINTING   PENER
MUZYKA   RASTAMANIEK I STAMARA1
26.10.2015   START GODZ. 20.00
PATERA   ŚWIĘTOKRZYSKO 36   WWA

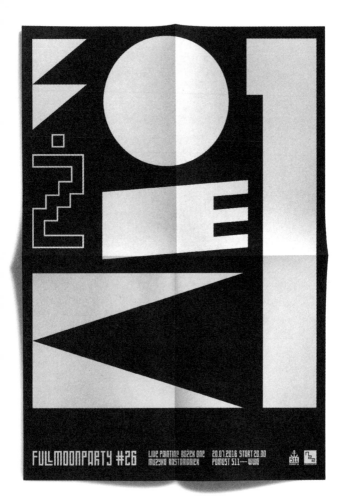

FULLMOONPARTY #26

LIVE PAINTING: BOZEK ONE
MUZYKA: KASTOMORIEK

20.07.2016 START 20.00
POMOST 511 — WWA

138

GREGOR

GĄSIOR

#22 full moon party LIVE PAINTING: GREGOR GĄSIOR
25.11.2015 — START godz. 20.00
poterą, Świętokrzyska 36, WWO

139

"Infographics without colours are sexy."

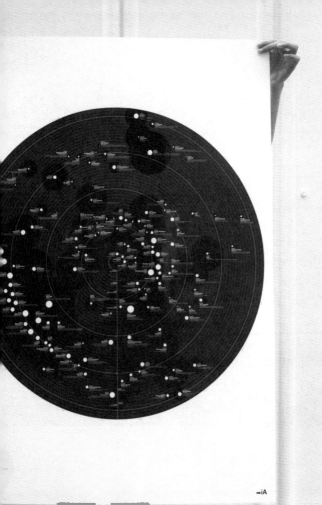

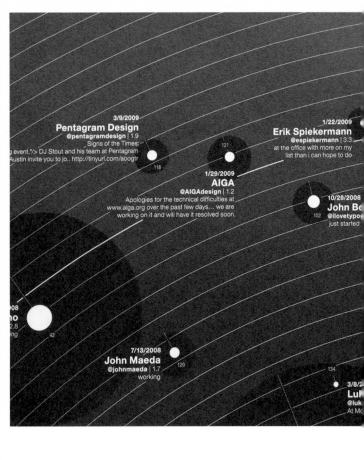

3/9/2009
Pentagram Design
@pentagramdesign | 1.9
Signs of the Times:
g event."/> DJ Stout and his team at Pentagram
Austin invite you to jo.. http://tinyurl.com/aoogtr

121

1/29/2009
AIGA
@AIGAdesign | 1.2
Apologies for the technical difficulties at
www.aiga.org over the past few days... we are
working on it and will have it resolved soon.

118

1/22/2009
Erik Spiekermann
@espiekermann | 3.3
at the office with more on my
list than i can hope to do

10/29/2008
John Be
@ilovetype
just started

102

008
no
2.8
ng

42

7/13/2008
John Maeda
@johnmaeda | 1.7
working

120

134

3/8/2
Lu
@luk
At M

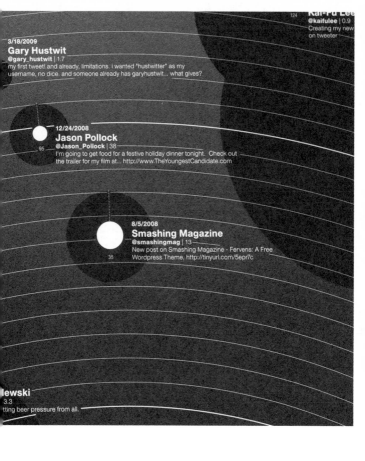

3/18/2009
Gary Hustwit
@gary_hustwit | 1.7
my first tweet! and already, limitations. i wanted "hustwitter" as my
username, no dice. and someone already has garyhustwit... what gives?

95
12/24/2008
Jason Pollock
@Jason_Pollock | 38
I'm going to get food for a festive holiday dinner tonight. Check out
the trailer for my film at... http://www.TheYoungestCandidate.com

8/5/2008
Smashing Magazine
@smashingmag | 13
35
New post on Smashing Magazine - Fervens: A Free
Wordpress Theme, http://tinyurl.com/5epr7c

lewski
3.3
tting beer pressure from all.

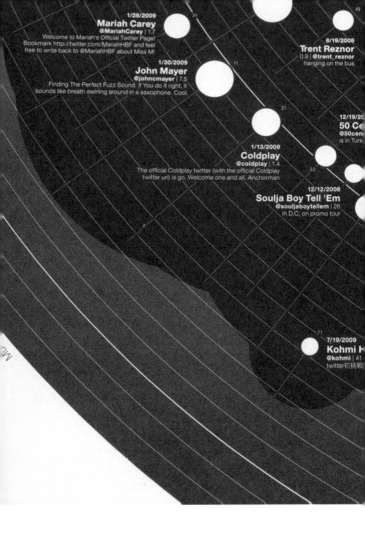

1/28/2009
Mariah Carey
@MariahCarey | 1.7
Welcome to Mariah's Official Twitter Page!
Bookmark http://twitter.com/MariahHBF and feel
free to write back to @MariahHBF about Miss M!

8/19/2008
Trent Reznor
0.9 | **@trent_reznor**
hanging on the bus

1/30/2009
John Mayer
@johncmayer | 7.5
Finding The Perfect Fuzz Sound. If You do it right, it
sounds like breath swirling around in a saxophone. Cool.

12/19/20
50 Ce
@50cen
is in Turk

1/13/2009
Coldplay
@coldplay | 1.4
The official Coldplay twitter (with the official Coldplay
twitter url) is go. Welcome one and all. Anchorman

12/12/2008
Soulja Boy Tell 'Em
@souljaboytellem | 26
In D.C. on promo tour

7/19/2009
Kohmi H
@kohmi | 41
twitter初挑戦

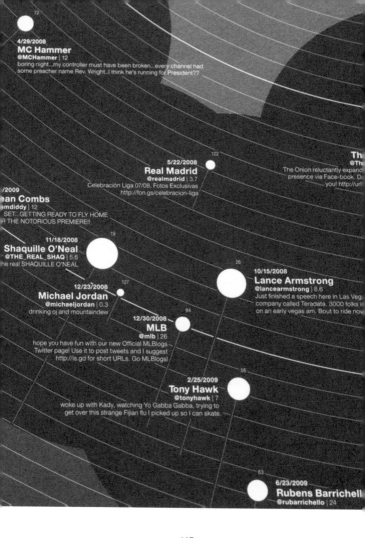

72
4/29/2008
MC Hammer
@MCHammer | 12
boring night...my controller must have been broken...every channel had
some preacher name Rev. Wright...I think he's running for President??

122
5/22/2008
Real Madrid
@realmadrid | 3.7
Celebración Liga 07/08. Fotos Exclusivas
http://fon.gs/celebracion-liga

Th
@Th
The Onion reluctantly expand
presence via Face-book. D
you! http://url

/2009
ean Combs
amdiddy | 12
SET...GETTING READY TO FLY HOME
R THE NOTORIOUS PREMIERE!!

19
11/18/2008
Shaquille O'Neal
@THE_REAL_SHAQ | 5.6
he real SHAQUILLE O'NEAL

26
10/15/2008
Lance Armstrong
@lancearmstrong | 8.6
Just finished a speech here in Las Veg
company called Teradata. 3000 folks in
on an early vegas am. Bout to ride now

127
12/23/2008
Michael Jordan
@michaeljordan | 0.3
drinking oj and mountaindew

94
12/30/2008
MLB
@mlb | 26
hope you have fun with our new Official MLBlogs
Twitter page! Use it to post tweets and I suggest
http://is.gd for short URLs. Go MLBlogs!

56
2/25/2009
Tony Hawk
@tonyhawk | 7
woke up with Kady, watching Yo Gabba Gabba, trying to
get over this strange Fijian flu I picked up so I can skate.

63
6/23/2009
Rubens Barrichell
@rubarrichello | 24

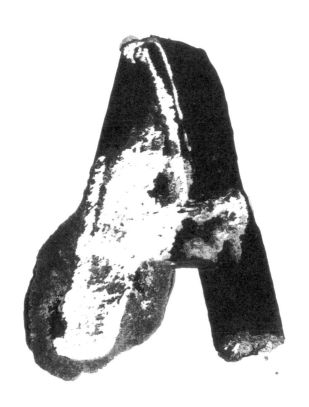

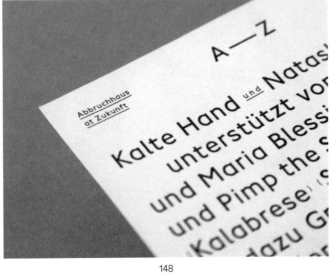

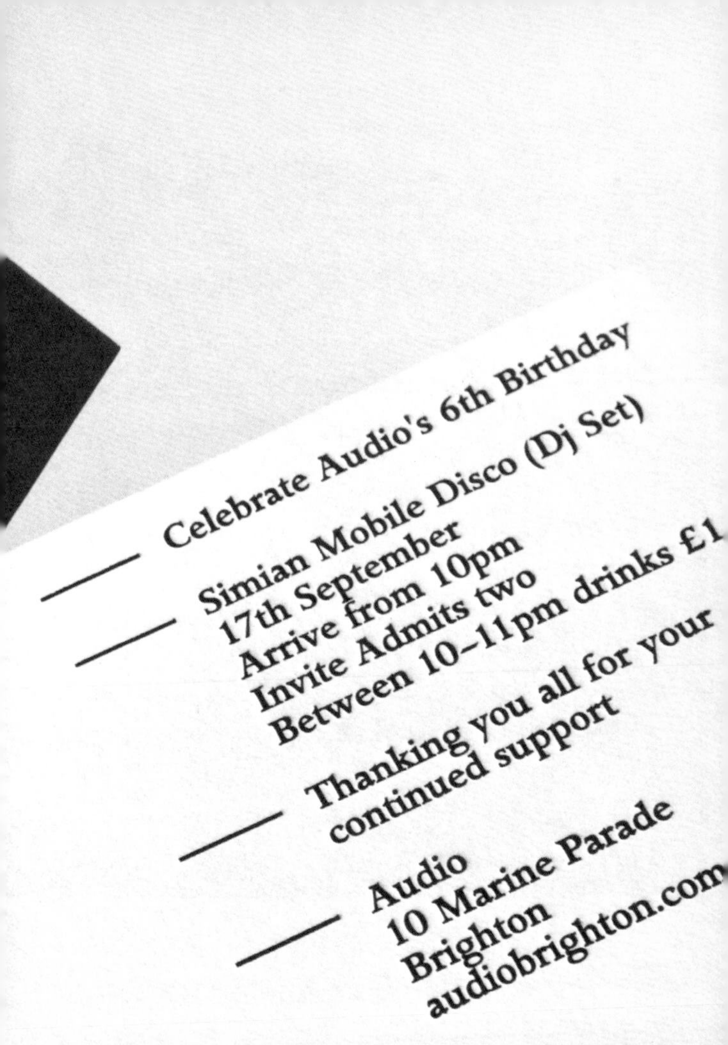

Celebrate Audio's 6th Birthday

Simian Mobile Disco (Dj Set)
17th September
Arrive from 10pm
Invite Admits two
Between 10–11pm drinks £1

Thanking you all for your
continued support

Audio
10 Marine Parade
Brighton
audiobrighton.com

— Celebrate Audio's Housewarming

— Foamo, Cagedbaby and Last Japan
18th September at 10pm
Invite Admits two

— Audio
5–6a Waterloo Terrace
Southampton
SO15 2AL
audiosouthampton.com
02380 630171

Audio·Launch

rate Audio's 6th Birthday
Mobile Disco (Dj Set)
otember
om 10pm
nits two
0–11pm drinks £1

u all for your
pport

de

n

155

Keep the shape poems coming... *

smel creative and strategic design studio
Wilgenweg 20 C / 1031 HV Amsterdam / The Netherlands
T (+31.20) 486 70 50 / F (+31.20) 486 70 51
www.smel.net / info@smel.net

KvK 34154305 Amst
Btw NL 809970211
ABN Amro Ams
IBAN NL89AB

Zijn we er klaar voor...?
*

eative and strategic design studio
eg 20 C / 1031 HV Amsterdam / The Netherlands

162

_From _Ground GmbH _Schyrenstr. 9 _81543 München _Germany
   _fon +49 (0) 89. 44 44 93 20 _buero@yourground.de _www.yourground.de

_With _Compliments _Greetings _Chocolatecake

_Ground

_Ground GmbH   Kon
Schyrenstr. 9   call
D-81543 München   mail

_Christian Haas   http:
_Geschäftsführer

_Ground

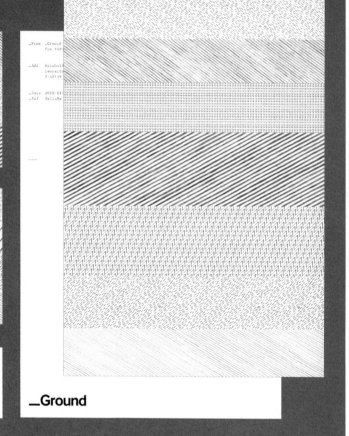

_From   _GroundB
        fon +49

_Add   Reinhold
        Leonard
        D-48159

_Date   2010-05
_Ref.   HelloMe

_Ground

168

169

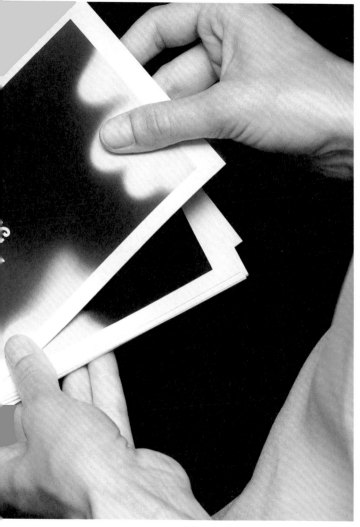

Jany Tremblay est une
photographe basée à Montréal
que vous pouvez joindre par
téléphone au 418 671 8458
ou par courriel à
info@janytremblay.com

Jany Tremblay est une
photographe basée à Montréal
que vous pouvez joindre par
téléphone au 418 671 8458
ou par courriel à
info@janytremblay.com

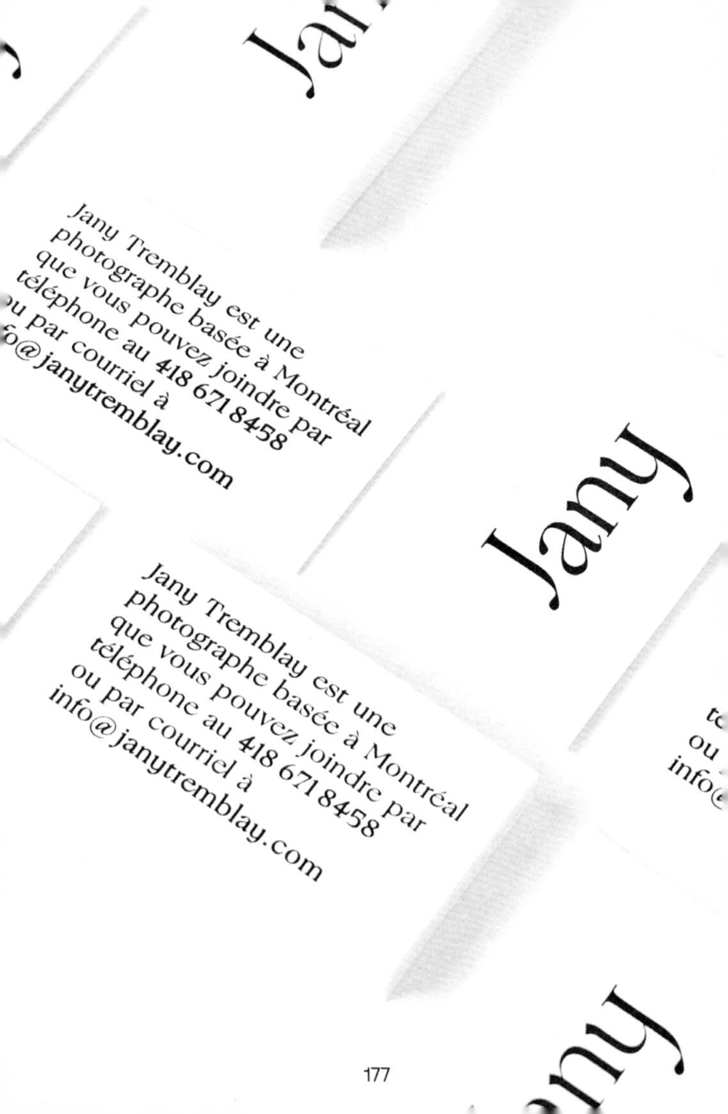

Jany

Jany Tremblay est une
photographe basée à Montréal
que vous pouvez joindre par
téléphone au 418 671 8458
ou par courriel à
fo@janytremblay.com

Jany

Jany Tremblay est une
photographe basée à Montréal
que vous pouvez joindre par
téléphone au 418 671 8458
ou par courriel à
info@janytremblay.com

to
ou
info@

Jany

Jany

3534, rue Lévis
Longueuil, QC J4L 2J3

(1) 877 3838
info@janytremblay.com

Regard vitreux d'un chihuahua
assis au pied d'une porte. *un chihuahua*

Jany Tremblay est une
photographe basée à Montréal
que vous pouvez joindre par
téléphone au 418 671 84...
ou par courriel à
info@janytremblay.c...

Plan rapproché d'...
souriant pris sur...

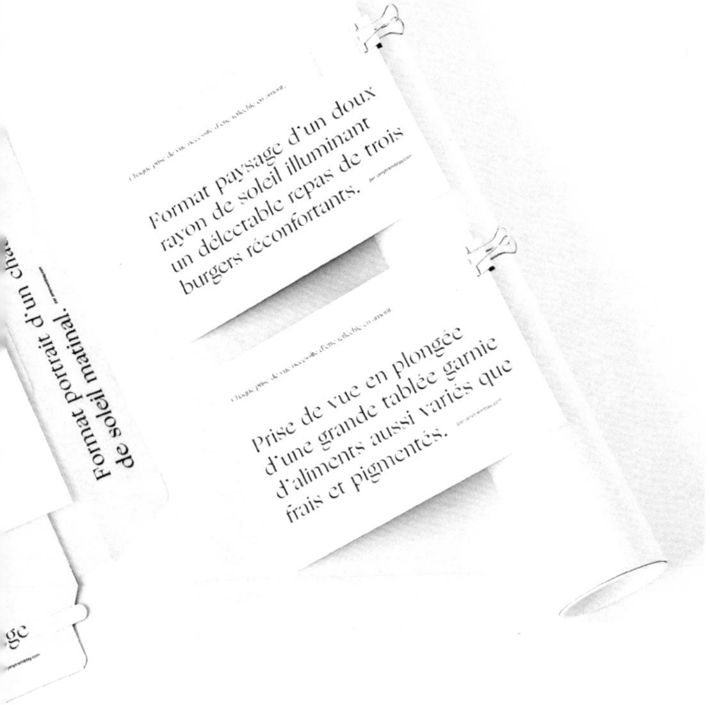

Format portrait d'un cha[...]
de soleil matinal. [...]

[...]ge

Chaque pièce de vue nouvelle d'art, soleil, etc. et avant

Format paysage d'un doux
rayon de soleil illuminant
un délectable repas de trois
burgers réconfortants. [...]

Chaque pièce de vue nouvelle d'art, soleil, etc. et avant

Prise de vue en plongée
d'une grande tablée garnie
d'aliments aussi variés que
frais et pigmentés. [...]

179

Jany

Format portrait d'un chaud rayon
de soleil matinal.

VOYAGEZ AVEC GOÛT

Choisir une courte profondeur de champ et créer des flous artistiques mettant en valeur l'élégance et l'éclat des plats. Utiliser un éclairage naturel servant à renforcer l'aspect authentique des clichés et ainsi mettre en appétit la clientèle.

PÉTONCLES DE LA NOUVELLE-ÉCOSSE
Réputation de la Nouvelle-Écosse poêlés, flambés au pastis, garnie de la noix de l'aneth.

LONGE DE PORC
Longe de porc au référence et béchamelle, laqués au miel, servis de pommes de terre rôties, jus.

RESPONSE:
ABILITY
TRANS-
MEDIALE.11
1 - 6 FEB
HAUS DER
KULTUREN
DER WELT

"UT transmediale.11 RESPONSE:ABILITY, 1 - 6 feb 2011, Haus der Kulturen der Welt, www.transmediale.de

KULTURSTIFTUNG DES BUNDES   KULTUR PROJEKTE BERLIN   medienboard   arte   DHB   der Freitag   DE:BUG   zitty   merklinz   www.Wall

"I perceive it as an all-or-nothing, straightforward message. It allows for a more thorough process of thinking when it comes to information priority."

anywhere in the world

anywhere in the world is the promotional poster of rui ribeiro.
He is trying to get a placement anywhere in the world as he is applying to a grant that will
allow him to be that ambitious.

Created on purpose for the INOV-ART program.
Promotional piece by Rui Ribeiro.
© 2011 www.cofseeing.com

a —
b

anywhere in the world

anywhere in the world is the promotional poster of rui ribeiro.
He is trying to get a placement anywhere in the world as he is applying to a grant that will
allow him to be that ambitious.

Created on purpose for the INOV-ART program.
Promotional piece by Rui Ribeiro.
© 2011 www.cofseeting.com

anywhere in the world

anywhere in the world is the promotional poster of rui ribeiro.
He is trying to get a placement anywhere in the world as he is applying to a grant that will
allow him to be that ambitious.

Created on purpose for the INOV-ART program.
Promotional piece by Rui Ribeiro.
© 2011 www.coffeeising.com

anywhere in the world

anywhere in the world is the promotional poster of rui ribeiro.
He is trying to get a placement anywhere in the world as he is applying to a grant that will
allow him to be that ambitious.

Created on purpose for the INOV-ART program.
Promotional piece by Rui Ribeiro.
© 2011 www.cofeeeling.com

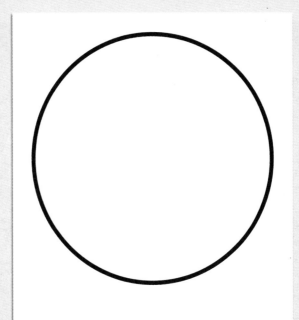

anywhere in the world

anywhere in the world is the promotional poster of rui ribeiro.
He is trying to get a placement anywhere in the world as he is applying to a grant that will
allow him to be stair ambitious.

Created on purpose for the INOV-ART program.
Promotional piece by Rui Ribeiro.
© 2011 www.coffeeing.com

BAD NEWS

WIESBADEN BIENNALE 23.8.–2.9.2018

NACHGENUTZTES THEATER   I...

CREATION (PICTURE...
FOR DORTA...

II/IV   33

NACHGENUTZTES THEATER

KÜNSTLER*IN
Milo Rau / IIPM & Campo

TITEL
FIVE EASY PIECES

ORT
Malsaal

TERMINE
01/09, 19.00
02/09, 15.00

UHRZEIT
19.00/
15.00

DAUER
90 Min

SPRACHE
Flämisch*

Seine Arbeiten zählen zu den wichtigsten
...eine Arbeiten zählen zu den wichtigsten
betrieb. „Five Easy Pieces" rückt
...führte mehrere
...in Gefäng...

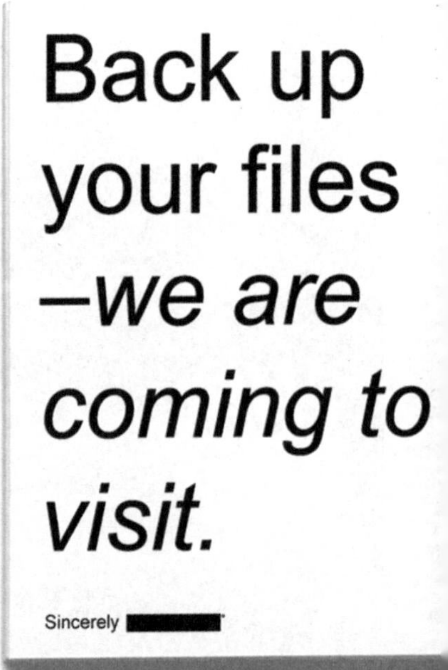

Back up your files —*we are coming to visit.*

Sincerely ███████

198

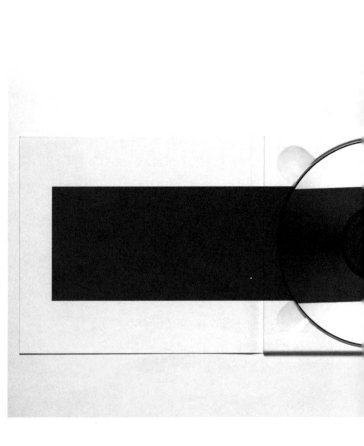

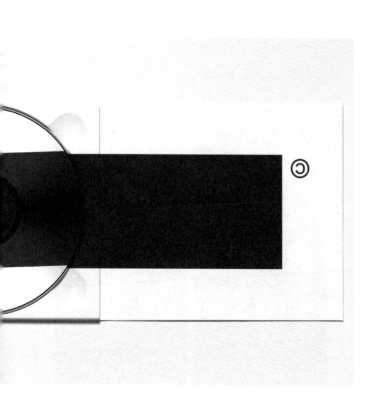

Foreign Rights
Frankfurt 2010
Non Fiction Books

Grupo Planeta

Foreign
Rights
Frankfurt 2010
Children

Grupo 🌐 Planeta

[GRUP 62]

Foreign Rights
Frankfurt 2010
Grup 62

Foreign
Rights
Frankfurt 2010
Fiction Books

Grupo Planeta

Spin

Wed
12.30pm–
The Rose Bowl
Portland Crescent
Leeds LS1 3HB

Admission: Free

Design by John Barton
www.johnbarton.co.uk

Screenprinted on Somerset Black 280gsm

Name:
Contents: Spin Lecture
Format: Poster
Date: Double sided A2
Design: 7th Dec
John Barton

ROBERT GELLER

AUTUMUN WINTER
2010 SHOW

ROBERT GELLER AUTUMN WINTER 20...

RSVP@FORCE-STEVENS.COM
LKFORCE-STEVENS.COM

FRIDAY
FEBRUARY 12 2010
8:00PM

EXIT ART
475 10TH AVENUE
AT 36TH STREET
NEW YORK NY 10018

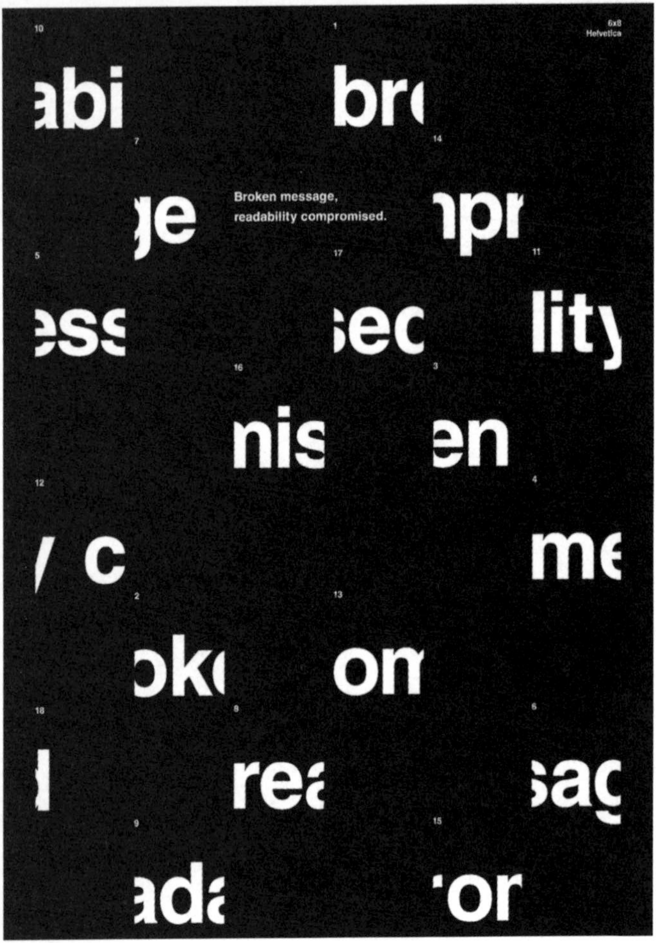

abi br(

je

**Broken message,
readability compromised.**

1pr

ess sec lity

nis en

/ c m(

ok(on

l rea sag

ad(or

10.
SEPTEMBER
2011
AB 20 UHR

ABBRUCH HAUS AT ZUKUNFT №2

MAHU
MITSUTEK & MARIA BLESSING
MONOME
SO YOU SO US
KALABRESE

VIDEOLOOPS
VON BARBARA SIGNER
SPECIAL VON
WWW.JAKOBSCHLAEPFER.COM
LESUNG VON STEVE LINDAUER
ST.GALLER WURST
VOM GRILL VON
UNSEREM GRILLMEISTER

DIENERSTRASSE 33, ZÜRICH
WWW.ZUKUNFT.CL
WWW.ABBRUCHHAUS.NET

МОСКОВСКИЙ
МУЗЕЙ ДИЗАЙНА
MOSCOW DESIGN
MUSEUM

Александра Санькова
организатор

ALEXANDRA SANKOVA
FOUNDER

T +7 926 245 9033
E SANKOVA@MOSCOWDESIGNMUSEUM.RU
W WWW.MOSCOWDESIGNMUSEUM.RU

219

МОСКОВСКИЙ
МУЗЕЙ ДИЗАЙНА
MOSCOW DESIGN
MUSEUM

Надежда Бакурадзе
организатор

NADEZHDA BAKURADZE
FOUNDER

T +7 926 204 6886
E BAKURADZE@MOSCOWDESIGNMUSEUM.RU
W WWW.MOSCOWDESIGNMUSEUM.RU

МОСКОВСКИЙ
МУЗЕЙ ДИЗАЙНА
MOSCOW DESIGN
MUSEUM

Валерий Патконен
организатор

VALERY PATKONEN
FOUNDER

T +7 495 729 1302
E PATKONEN@MOSCOWDESIGNMUSEUM.RU
W WWW.MOSCOWDESIGNMUSEUM.RU

223

"Black and white enable other things to become visible and at the same time reduce them to their essential."

228

231

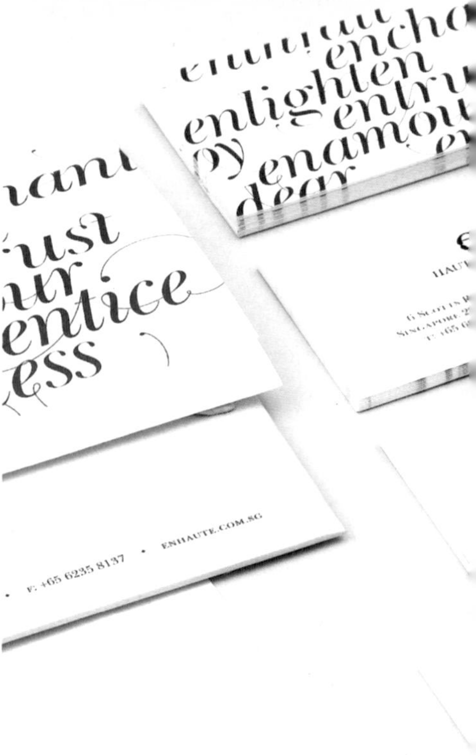
enlighten
entice
F: +65 6235 8137 • ENHAUTE.COM.SG

enthrall
enchant
enlighten
enjoy
entrust
enamour.
endear
entice
endless
en
HAUTE JOAILLERIE
wishlist

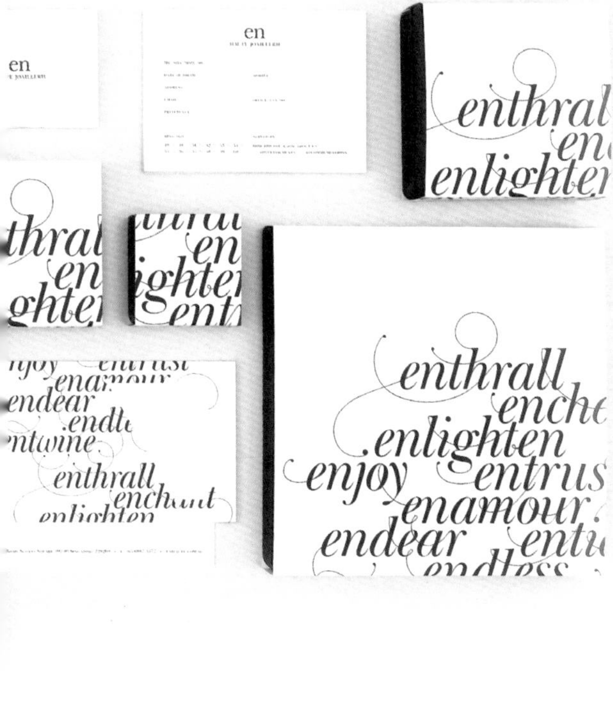
en
en
enthrall
enlighten
enjoy
endear
enamour
entwine

DESK IDEA

deskidea.com

deskidea.com

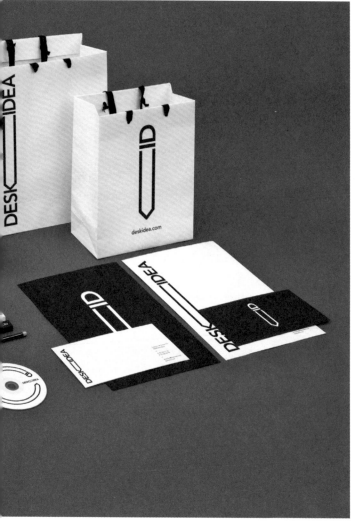

240

"Black and white suit bold graphics and are visually more powerful and cost-effective at the same time."

SIGNAL NO.1 HAS BEEN ISSUED. IT IS JUST A STAND-BY SIGNAL. WE WILL CONTINUE TO BRAINSTORM AND BLOW YOUR MIND AWAY. GET READY FOR THE CYCLONE. CLOSE YOUR WINDOWS AND OPEN YOUR MIND.

BLOW IS A HONG KONG BASED DESIGN STUDIO FOUNDED BY BEN LO IN MAY 2010. SPECIALIZE IN BRANDING, IDENTITIES, VISUAL, ENVIRONMENT

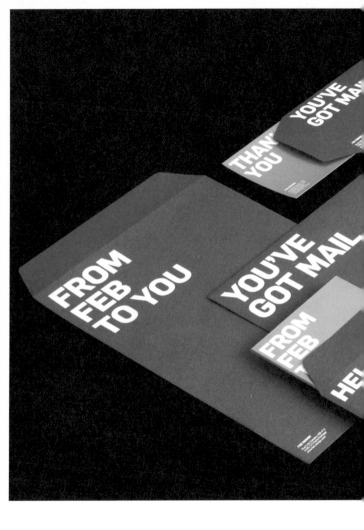

248

BY FEB
TO YOU

WE
ARE
FEB

NICE
TO
MEET
YOU

249

253

5550, rue Fullum
Suite 202
Montréal, Qc
H2G 2H4

info
idoinebio.com   @

                                 t. 514.383.2254

Montréal, Québec

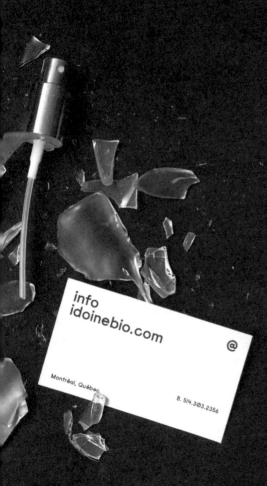

info
idoinebio.com

@

Montréal, Québec

B. 514.303.2356

260

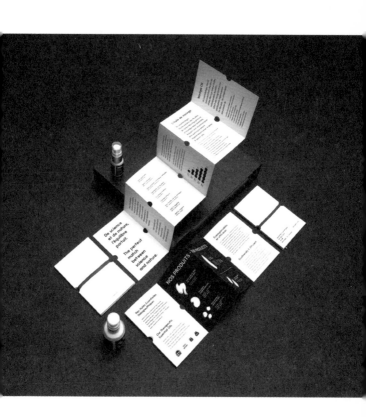

261

Annantalon taidekeskus,
Annankatu 30, Helsinki
Annegårdens konstcentrum,
Annegatan 30, Helsingfors

Näyttely avoinna
Utställningen öppen
5. 4.–14. 12. 2008
ark. klo 9–20, la–su klo 11–17
vard. kl. 9–20, lör–sön. kl. 11–17

VAPAA PÄÄSY / FRITT INTRÄDE

ANNA MUN OLLA:

näyttely- & tapahtumakokonaisuus

—————————————————— ●

ANNA MUN OLLA
— näyttely & tapahtumat

LÅT MIG VARA
— utställningar & evenemang

Anna mun olla on oikean mittainen näyttely- ja tapahtumakokonaisuus, joka korvaa näkökulmaa Pekka Elomaan ohjemiä Lapsi
ry:n. Helsingin kaupunginteatteri ja nuorisoryhmä koettaa kanssa ennakoimaan kokemus...

Lät mig vara är en av Lapsis ry:n utställnings- och evenemangs som genomförts under kalenderåret 2008...

Lisätietoja vastaava kulttuurituottaja
Liisa Pentula, puh. 310/37174.

Näyttely- ja tapahtumakokonaisuuden toteuttaa yhdessä Annantalon taidekeskuksen kanssa valtakunnan Pekka Elomaa, Lapsi ry, Kohalo-keskus ja Leijonaosasto ry.

Programmet för utställnings- och evenemangshelheten låt mig vara kan erhållas på internet www.annantalo.fi.

Närmare information ger ansvarig kulturproducent Liisa Pentula, tfn 310 37174.

I samarbete Annegårdens konstcentrum,
fotograf Pekka Elomaa, Lapsi rf, Kohalo-center och Leijonaosasto rf.

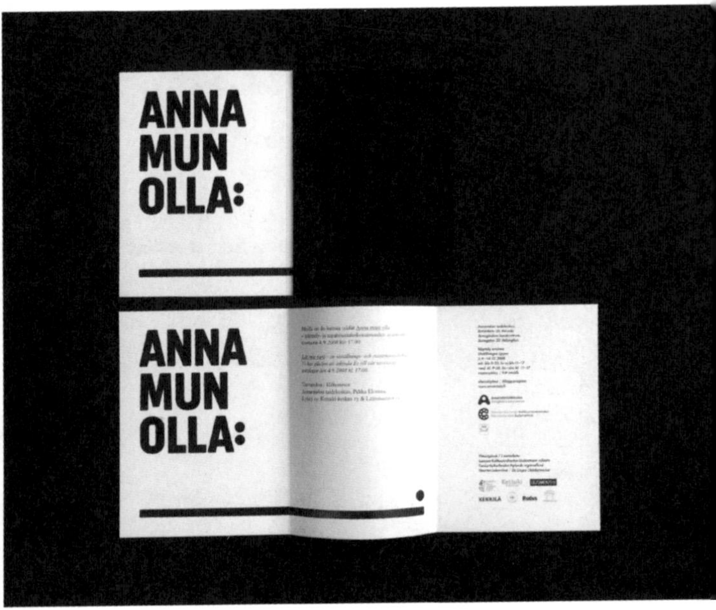
ANNA
MUN
OLLA:
ANNA
MUN
OLLA:

269

e Ultimate Paper

ohawk Superfine is the
est printing paper made
day. No other paper
s the same reputation
r quality, consistency and
iformity. Superfine
spires great design with
superb formation, lush
ctility, archival quality and
neless appeal.

Superfine
is craftmenship.

Introduction

Tai Tak Takeo Fine Paper in collaboration with Toby Ng Design is pleased to present "Superfine Defined". The conceptual collection is embodied in this miniature cubic booklet designed and made with exquisite precision and delicacy. It showcases the diverse interpretive work from a multitude of Hong Kong young creatives, capturing the definition of 'superfine'. Between text and image, a blur occurs as each is altered by the other. Mohawk Superfine paper provides a rich canvas for infinite possibilities, epitomizing the transformative power of medium and subject.

"Black and white make a perfect contrast to the vibrancy of art, especially on digital platforms."

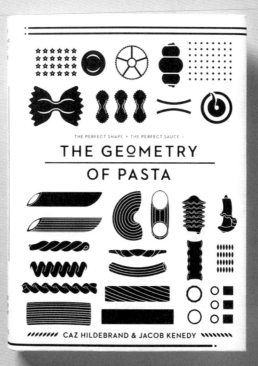

THE PERFECT SHAPE • THE PERFECT SAUCE

THE GEOMETRY
OF PASTA

CAZ HILDEBRAND & JACOB KENEDY

THE PERFECT SHAPE · THE PERFECT SAUCE ·

THE GEOMETRY
OF PASTA

CAZ HILDEBRAND & JACOB KENEDY

GRADO

PS500e
Professional Series

282

'53

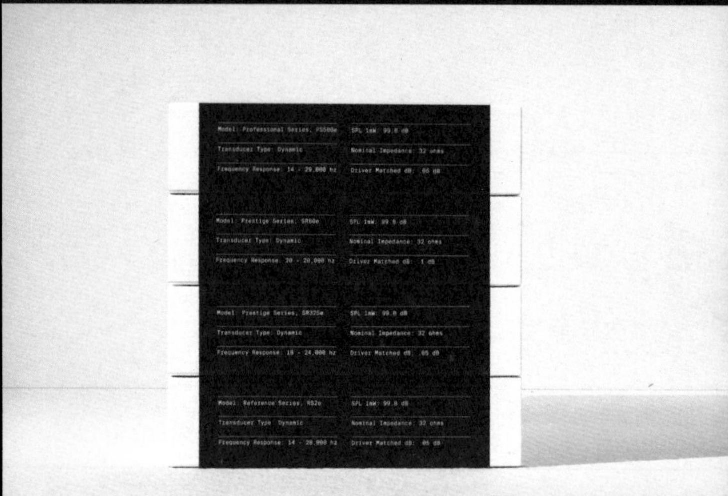
Model: Professional Series, PS500e
SPL 1mW: 99.8 dB
Transducer Type: Dynamic
Nominal Impedance: 32 ohms
Frequency Response: 14 - 29,000 hz
Driver Matched dB: .05 dB
Model: Prestige Series, SR80e
SPL 1mW: 99.8 dB
Transducer Type: Dynamic
Nominal Impedance: 32 ohms
Frequency Response: 20 - 20,000 hz
Driver Matched dB: 1 dB
Model: Prestige Series, SR325e
SPL 1mW: 99.8 dB
Transducer Type: Dynamic
Nominal Impedance: 32 ohms
Frequency Response: 18 - 24,000 hz
Driver Matched dB: .05 dB
Model: Reference Series, RS2e
SPL 1mW: 99.8 dB
Transducer Type: Dynamic
Nominal Impedance: 32 ohms
Frequency Response: 14 - 28,000 hz
Driver Matched dB: .05 dB

Family run for six decades
in Brooklyn, New York

SPL 1mW: 99.8 dB

Nominal Impedance: 32 ohms

Driver Matched dB: .1 dB

Melanie

Hi!

Jan

DESCRYPTOR

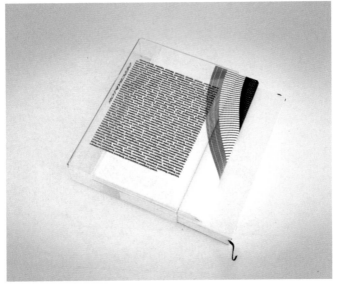

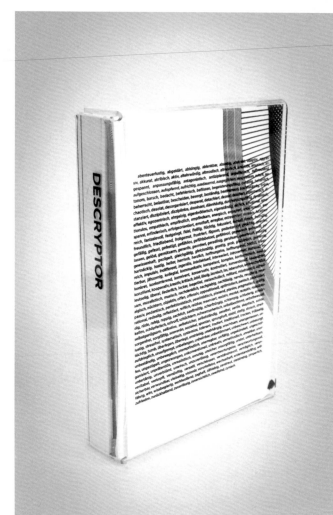

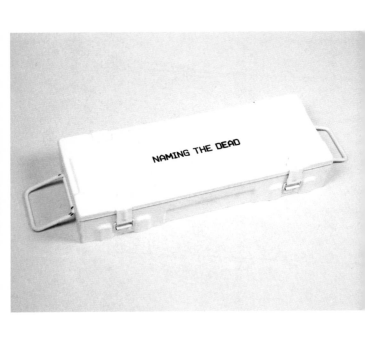

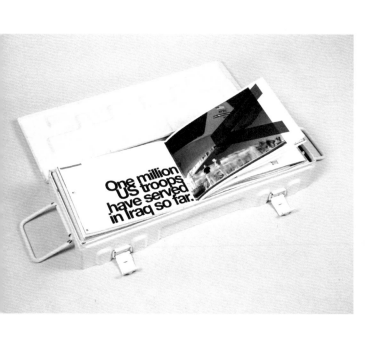

One million
US troops
have served
in Iraq so far.

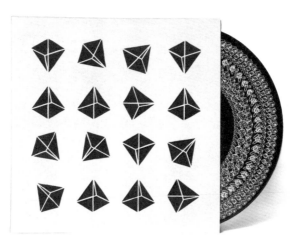

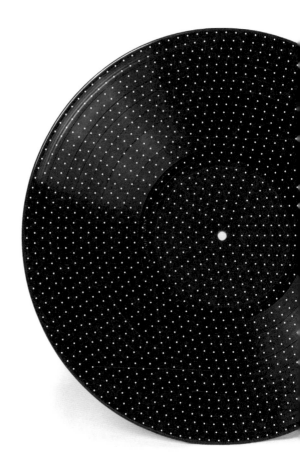

THE
INDISCREETS
—

PINS
AND
THREADS

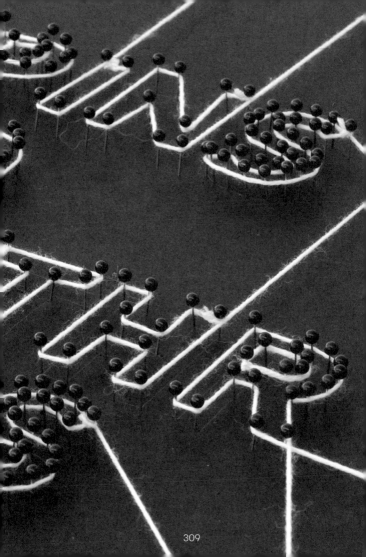

THE
INDISCREETS

THE
INDISCREETS

01 THE BURNING ROOM
02 PINS AND THREADS
03 ARTIFICIAL
04 MINOR PROBLEMS
05 NEAR
06 MOST RULES ARE STUPID
07 INSERT DISC
08 A TERRIFIC TRANSITION
09 ATTACK OF THE ARCHITECTS
10 SWEEPING FLOORS
11 LIKE A HUNT
12 PATHOS

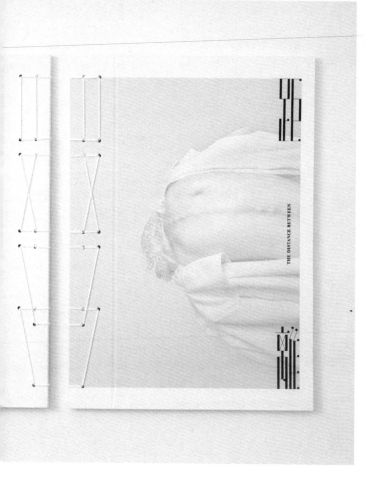

THE DISTANCE BETWEEN

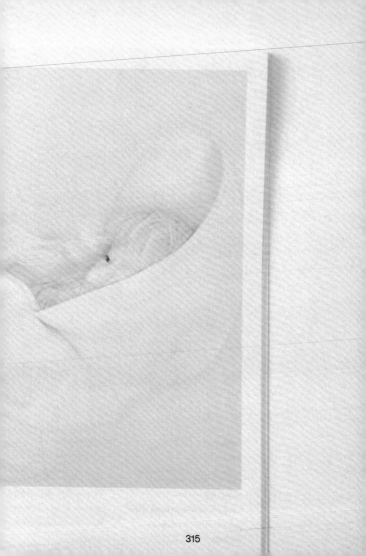

"Visually, words are at their best in black or white."

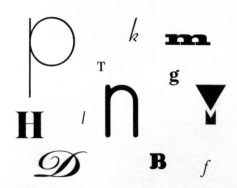

THE NECESSITY
OF SILENCE
*Film Composers Talk about
the Art and Theory of Writing Music
for Cinema*

羅展鳳 著

必要的靜默

世界電影音樂創作談

華語世界第一本有關外國電影音樂的「作者論」著作，
集十三位風格迥異大師級音樂家與創作者的訪談及講座紀錄。

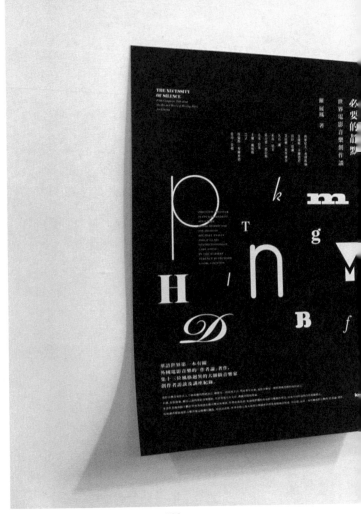

遙遠
星球的
孩子

CHILDREN FROM THE
DISTANT PLANET

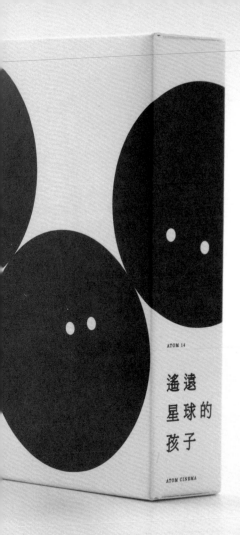

ATOM 14

遠
遙 球 的
星
孩 子

ATOM CINEMA

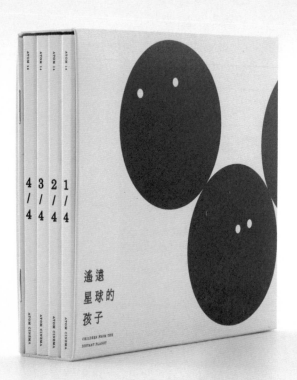

遙遠
星球的
孩子

CHILDREN FROM THE
DISTANT PLANET

遙遠
星球的
孩子
CHILDREN FROM THE
DISTANT PLANET

3／4

4／4
自閉症之謎

遙遠
星球的
孩子
CHILDREN FROM THE
DISTANT PLANET
4 / 4

2 / 4

Eye
of
the
Times

Eye
of
the
Times

Centennial
Images
of
Taiwan

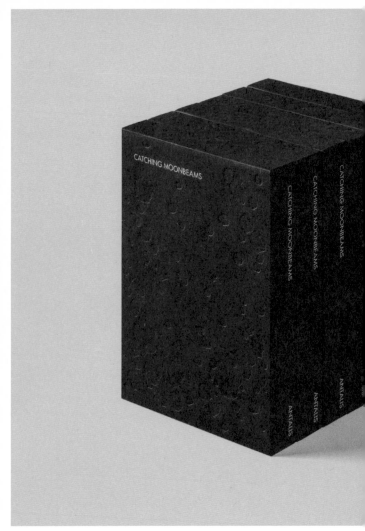

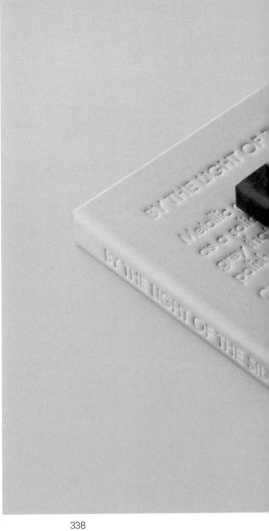

BY THE LIGHT OF

Metallic
as a sol
grey, fro
polish
c

BY THE LIGHT OF

BY THE LIGHT OF THE SIL

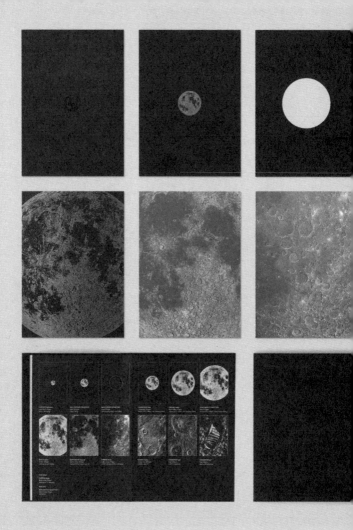

344

345

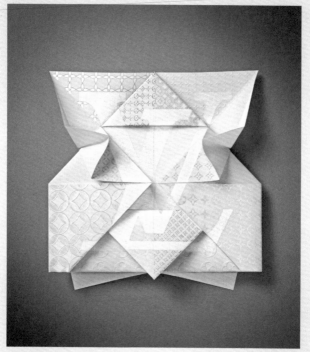

Shinsaibashi Plaza bldg 1F 3-12-12 Minami Senba Chuo-ku, Osaka   www.louisvuitton.com

LOUIS VUITTON

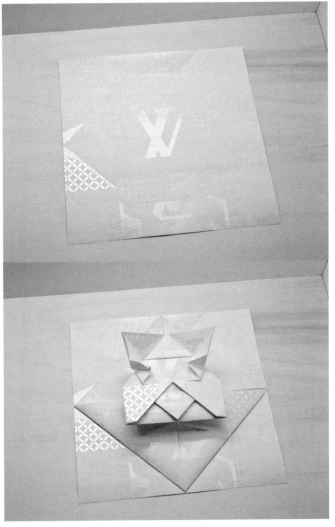

348

349

WASSILY KANDINSKY
ÜBER DAS GEISTIGE
IN DER KUNST 1911

LANGE TRÜ-
UND MANCHE
N UND MANCHE
GANZ ZERFLIESSEN,
EINEN SCHWACHEN,
ENTKRÄFTETEN
KLANG HINTERLAS-
SEN

353

EINE
Einesigns Limited
1 Cloudesley Road St Leonards on Sea East Sussex TN37 6JN
T +44 (0)7738 856 770 E ben1977@me.com W einesigns.co.uk
Company No: 07444427

EINE
Einesigns Limited
1 Cloudesley Road St Leonards on Sea East Sussex TN37 6JN
T +44 (0)7738 836 770 E bena1977@me.com W einesigns.co.uk
Company No. 07444427

EINE
Einesigns Limited 1 Cloudesley Road
St Leonards on Sea East Sussex TN37 6JN
T +44 (0)7738 836 770 E bena1977@me.com
W einesigns.co.uk

357

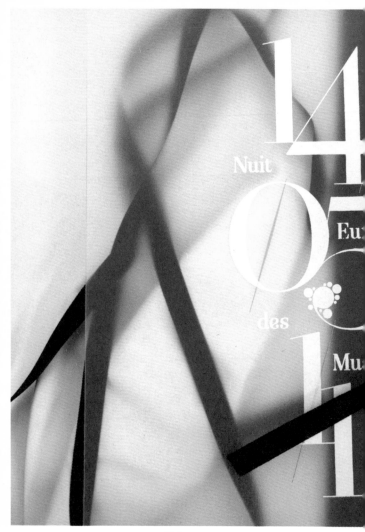

Nuit

14

O

Eu...

des

Mu...

14

Musée des Beaux-Arts de Caen

Nuit

4
0
5

Européenne

des

Musées

4

INVITATION / MURMURE
à la nuit tombée...

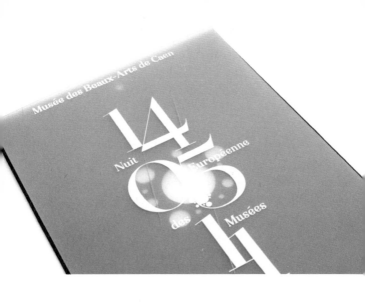

Musée des Beaux-Arts de Caen

14 05
Nuit Européenne des Musées

14 05
Nuit Européenne des Musées

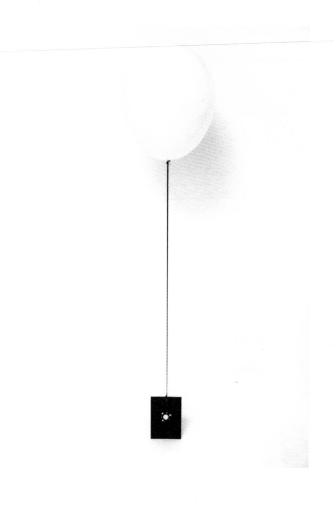

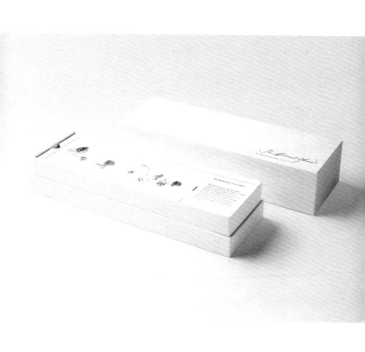

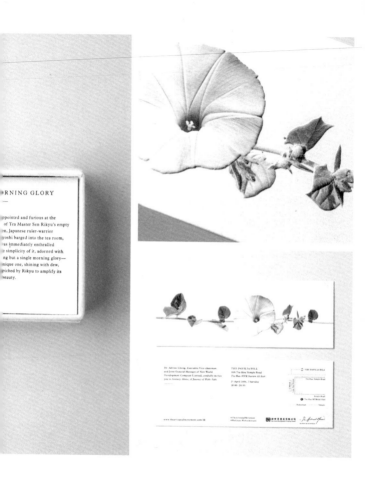

MORNING GLORY

Disappointed and furious at the sight of Tea Master Sen Rikyu's empty garden, Japanese ruler-warrior Hideyoshi barged into the tea room, and was immediately enthralled by the simplicity of it, adorned with nothing but a single morning glory— the unique one, shining with dew, handpicked by Rikyu to amplify its beauty.

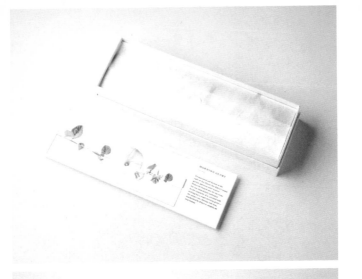

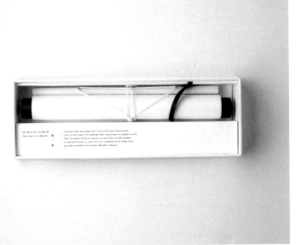

BLANC

Brasserie mediterrània
amb influències asiàtiques

Brasserie mediterránea
con influencias asiáticas

Mediterranean brasserie
with Asian influences

Cuina ininterrompuda de 7 h a 23 h
Menú executiu de dilluns a divendres
Sopar a la carta i barra de martinis

Cocina ininterrumpida de 7 h a 23 h
Menú ejecutivo de lunes a viernes
Cena a la carta y barra de martinis

Kitchen open daily from 7 am till 11 pm
Executive lunch menu from Monday to Friday
A la carte dinner & martini bar

BLANC
Mandarin Oriental, Barcelona
Passeig de Gràcia, 38-40
08007 Barcelona
T +34 93 151 88 88
mobcn-blanc@mohg.com
www.restaurantblanc.com

MANDARIN ORIENTAL
BARCELONA

Jean Luc Figueras

373

3LANC
brasserie & gastrobar

VINOS BLANCOS POR COPAS
WHITE WINES FOR GLASS

D.O. Penedès
Crisalys de Torelló Xarel.lo 2010   6,00 €
Can Credo 2008   6,90 €

D.O. Costers del Segre
Els Eixaders Chardonnay 2008   7,00 €

D.O. Rías Baixas
Zios de Lusco 2010   6,00 €

V.D.T. Castilla y León
Quinta Apolonia 2009   6,00 €

MANDARIN ORIENTAL
BARCELONA

3LANC
brasserie & gastrobar

ESPUMOSOS POR COPAS
ESPUMOSOS FOR GLASS

D.O. Cava
Mont-Marçal Extremarium   5,00 €

A.O.C. Champagne
Bollinger Spécial Cuvée   13,00 €
Bollinger Rosé   28,00 €

VINOS ROSADOS POR COPAS
ROSE WINES FOR GLASS

D.P. Terra Alta
Mas Amor 2010 Rosado   7,00 €

A.O.C. Côtes de Provence
Domaine d'Ott Château
de Selle Coeur de Grain 2010   11,00 €

MANDARIN ORIENTAL
BARCELONA

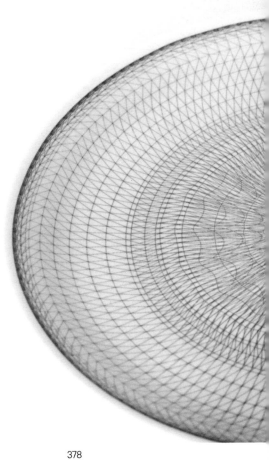

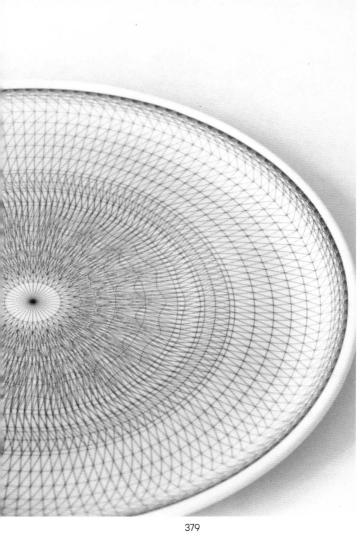

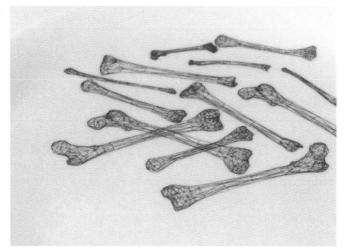

382

NEGRE

D.O.EMPORDÀ

2011

DE JORDI OLIVER CONTI

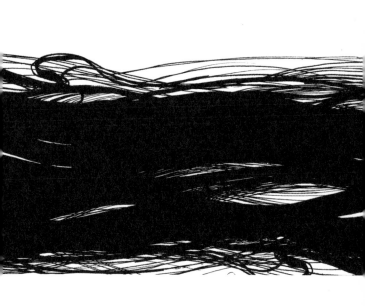

五十
代国

 WUDAI SHIGUO **WUDAI SHIGUO**

今作仲秋之餅
廣傳多路英豪
以成盟約
大日近矣、哲必繼聲而起
與爾成陣

 歡迎、候教

WUDAI SHIGUO ❀ **WUDAI SHIGUO** ❀ **WUDAI SHIGUO**

402

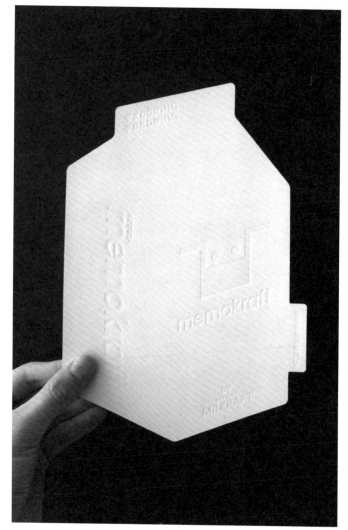

410

"Printing black on black and white on white always give a classic feel."

414

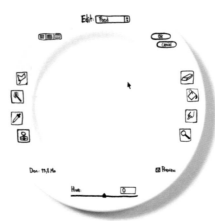

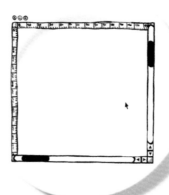

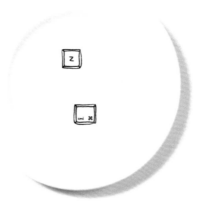

419

Greece
is
for lovers

Greece
is
for lovers

Greece
is
for lovers

FLAVOUR OF
THE MONTH
A current, but
temporary craving

A heavenly concoction
of a paperweight:
Cool and refreshing minty
white marble, snuggly
enveloped in smooth Tyvek,
fitted on a chromed brass
popsicle stick.

www.greeceisforlovers.com

FLAVOUR OF
THE MONTH
A current, but
temporary craving

A heavenly concoction
of a paperweight:
Cool and refreshing minty
white marble, snuggly
enveloped in smooth Tyvek,
fitted on a chromed brass
popsicle stick.

www.greeceisforlovers.com

BEYOND
DESSERT

426

BEYOND
DESSERT

BEYOND
DESSERT

"We live in colours. Being monochromatic is a distinction, however."

437

439

"It's striking and graphic, cross gender and harbours less bias."

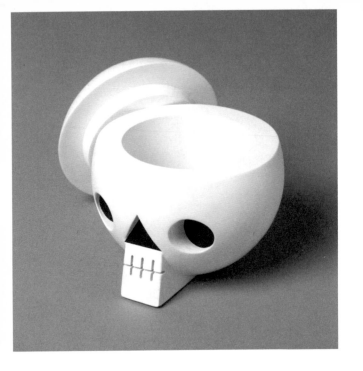

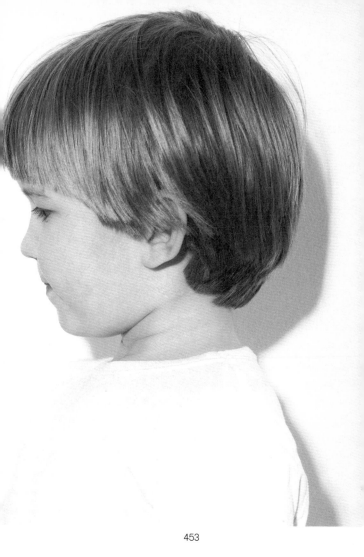

457

458

459

Hierony
The Bunny of the

A limited ...on porc
designed b... ...rville / p...
...as & 3 int
contains H... ...e / jeremy
t...

466

nymus
t the Apocalypse

n porcelain sculpture
yville / produced by Toykyo
us & 3 internal organ friends
.be / jeremyville.com

469

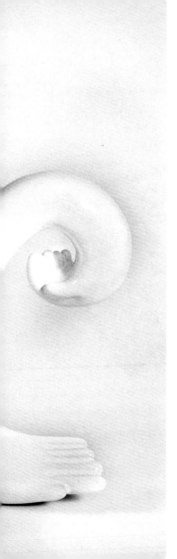

473

Limited edition T-shirt / 200
Design by Büro X
Illustration by Oers Budion
www.oners.com.kr

479

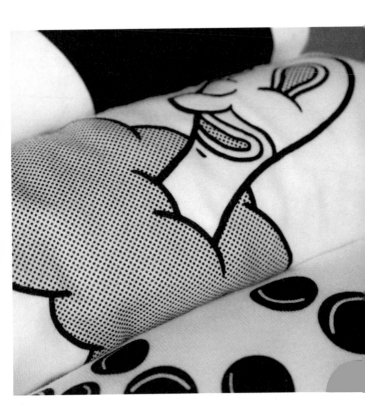

"Black is often a reference to the photography world. A presence to the eye that no other colour can provide."

485

01 / AMP ODYSSEY   02 / 33-RPM RECORD   03 / C90 CASSETTE TAPE   04 / C60 CASSETTE TAPE   05 / SONY STEREO WALKMAN   06 / BRAUN SK55   07 / 1/4" CABLE   08 / HITACHI TRK - 8800   09 / ELH 17

489

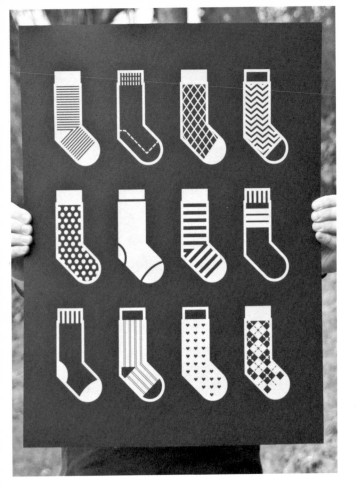

492

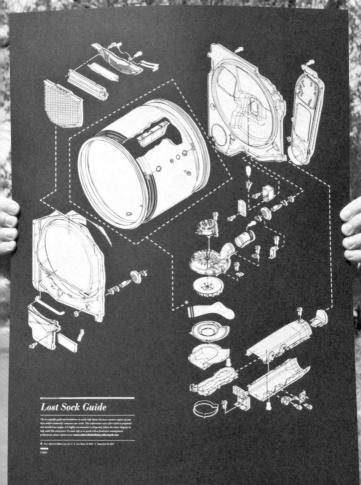

Lost Sock Guide

This is a specific guide and breakdown to really help locate the most common regions of your dryer which commonly consume rare socks. This unfortunate sister often leads to perpetual not matched sox singles. It is highly recommended to frequently follow the eleven diagram to help void this annoyance. For more info or to speak with a frustration management professional, please contact us at: www.wheretheballlaundrysockmade.com

7 2017

498

499

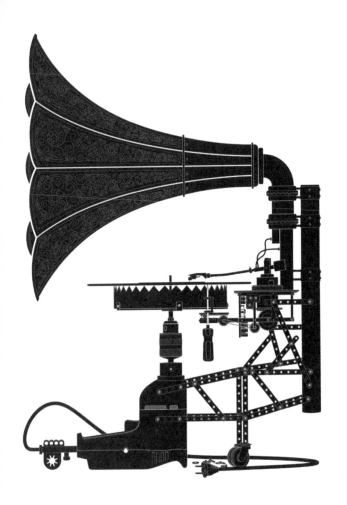

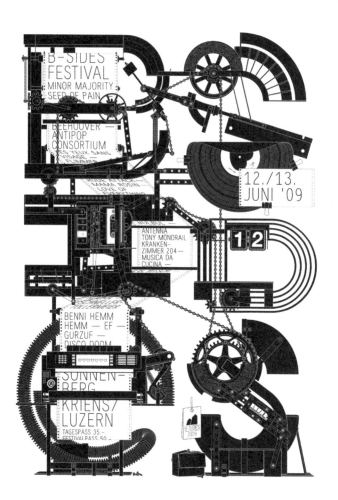

B-SIDES
FESTIVAL
MINOR MAJORITY
SEED OF PAIN

BEETHOOVER —
ANTIPOP
CONSORTIUM

12./13.
JUNI '09

12

BENNI HEMM
HEMM — EF —
GURZUF —
DISCO DOOM

SONNEN-
BERG
KRIENS/
LUZERN
TAGESPASS 35.-
FESTIVAL PASS 50.-

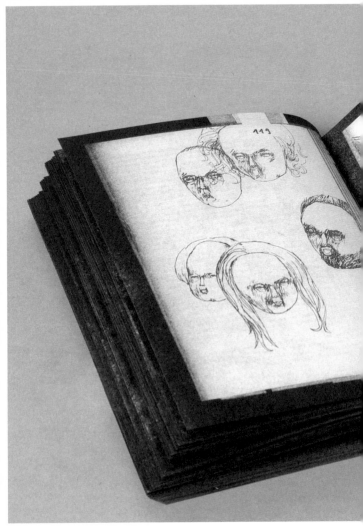

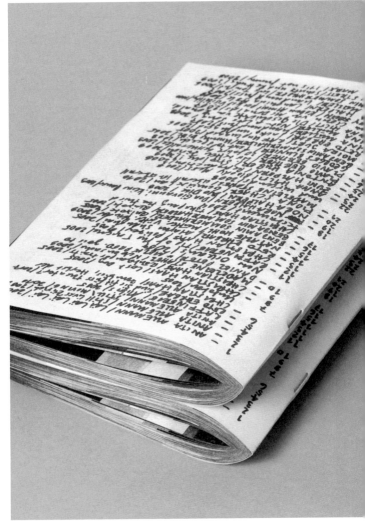

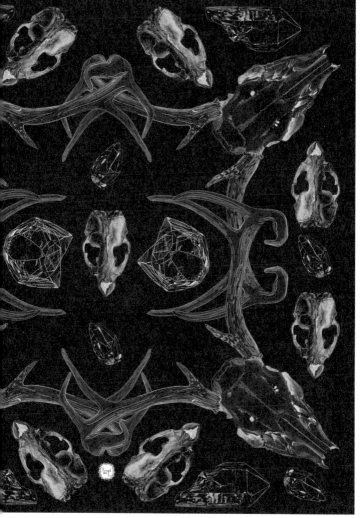

507

508

518

EAN PIERRE LE DOUCHE

LIMITED EDITION PORCELAIN SCULPTURE

ESIGNED BY *Parra*

PRODUCED & PUBLISHED BY CASE STUDYO 2012

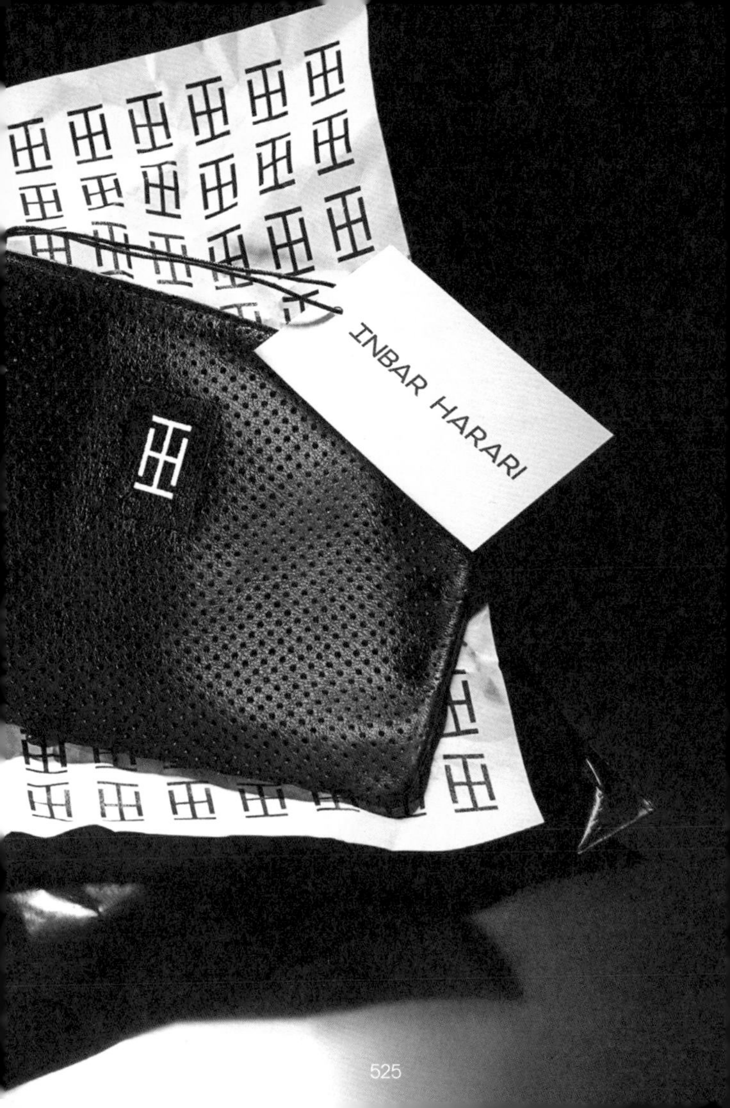
INBAR HARARI

INBAR HARARI

528

534

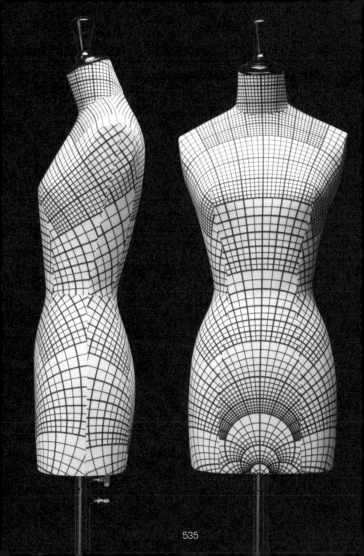

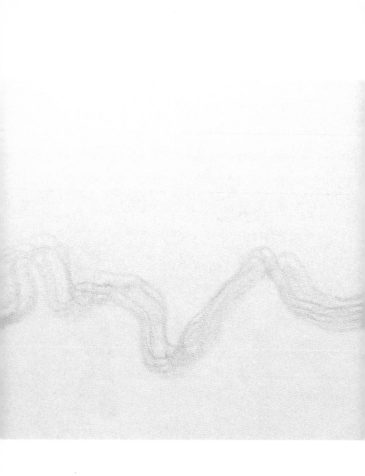

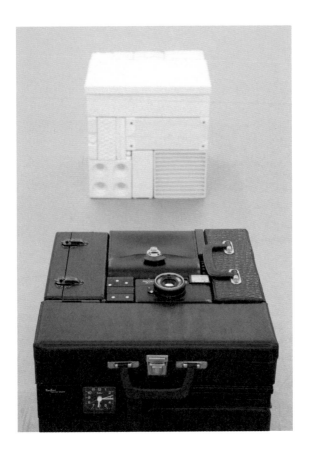

544

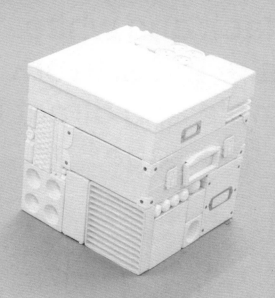

"Black and white make the artwork simple and direct in its message."

GF

KAREN
WALKER

THE
TEA ROOM

HERE AT THE TEA ROOM WE'RE FAMOUS FOR OUR SOUPS

LAST WINTER'S FAVOURITES INCLUDED: TAMARIND, LENTIL & CORIANDER, TUSCAN BEAN & WINTER VEGETABLE, KUMARA, SWEET CHILI & LEEK. FRESH SOUP WILL BE SERVED DAILY FROM APRIL 01

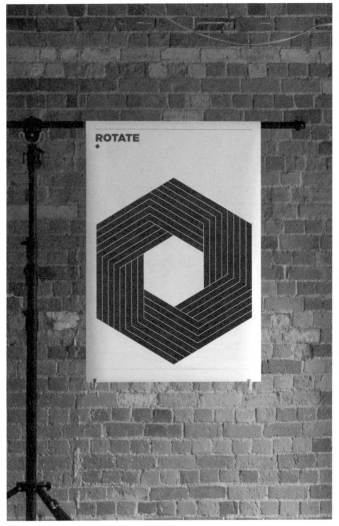

553

554

DETROIT
UNDERGROUND
· HIGHWAYS ·
33RPM

556

Transition
Premiere 4.9.14, 20:30
5. 9. – 6.9.14, 20:30
7.9.14, 18:00

Ort   Tickets 15/10€   A production made at studio laborgras.

Dock 11   Ticketreservation: laborgras is supported by:
Kastanienallee 79   www.reservix.de   Der Regierende Bürgermeister von Berlin
10435 Berlin   studio@laborgras.com   Senatskanzlei - Kulturelle Angelegenheiten.

Ambulo ergo sum —
ich laufe, also bin ich
11.9. – 12.9.15, 20:30
13.9.15, 18:00

Ort   Tickets 15/10€   A production made at studio laborgras.

Studio 14   Ticketreservation   laborgras is supported by:
Uferstr. 8   www.reservix.de oder   Der Regierende Bürgermeister von Berlin
13357 Berlin   studio@laborgras.com   Senatskanzlei - Kulturelle Angelegenheiten.

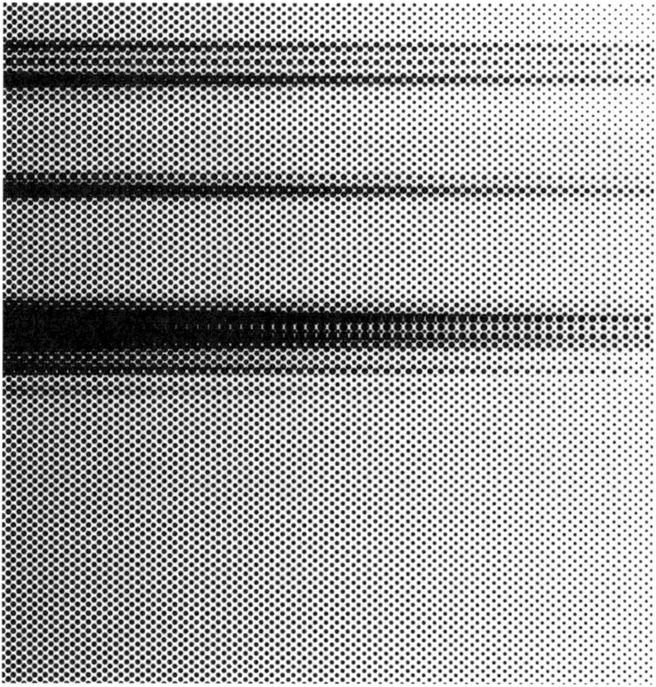

David Hernandez & Collaborators
For Movement's Sake
at Dock 11
25.02. 2016, 19:00
26.02. 2016, 19:00

Tickets 15/10€   Production laborgras.com

Ticketreservation
030-35120312
ticket@dock11-berlin.de

Studio laborgras is supported by:
Der Regierende Bürgermeister von Berlin
Senatskanzlei - Kulturelle Angelegenheiten.

Studio laborgras presents
Interference — An Evening of 3 Pieces
Choreographed by Rossella Canciello,
Rosalind Masson, Arianna Rodeghiero
December 3rd, 2016, 20:00

Tickets 12/9€

Ticket Reservation
T 030-695.051.83
studio@laborgras.com

Studio laborgras

Paul-Lincke-Ufer 44A
2nd backyard
10999 Berlin

Production at laborgras.com

Studio laborgras is supported by:
Der Regierende Bürgermeister von Berlin
Senatskanzlei - Kulturelle Angelegenheiten.

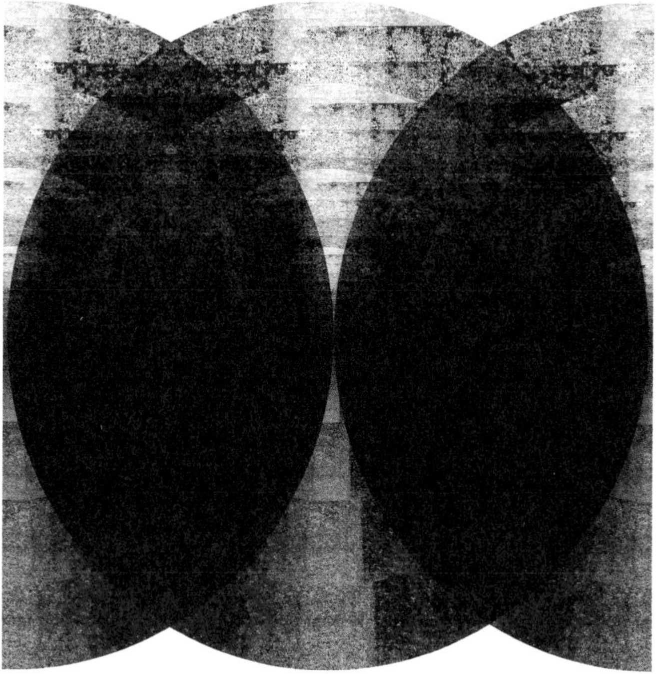

Neubau

Red, Coffee & Fog
by Nina Berclaz
Spectral Schematics
by Lea Pischke
19.2. & 20.2.16, 20:00

David He
For Move
at Dock
25.02. 20
26.02. 20

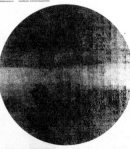

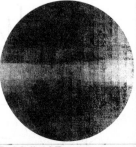

Red, Coffee & Fog
by Nina Berclaz
Spectral Schematics
by Lea Pischke
19.2. & 20.2.16, 20:00

Red, Coffee & Fog
by Nina Berclaz
Spectral Schematics
by Lea Pischke
19.2. & 20.2.16, 20:00

David He
For Move
at Dock
25.02. 20
26.02. 20

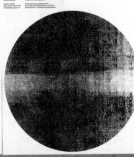

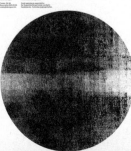

David Hernandez & Collaborators |
For Movement's Sake
at Dock 11
25.02. 2016, 19:00
26.02. 2016, 19:00

David Hernandez & Collaborators |
For Movement's Sake
at Dock 11
25.02. 2016, 19:00
26.02. 2016, 19:00

David Hernandez & Collaborators |
For Movement's Sake
at Dock 11
25.02. 2016, 19:00
26.02. 2016, 19:00

David Hernandez & Collaborators |
For Movement's Sake
at Dock 11
25.02. 2016, 19:00
26.02. 2016, 19:00

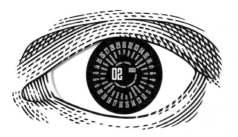

РАВЕНСТВО
www.ravenstvo.ru

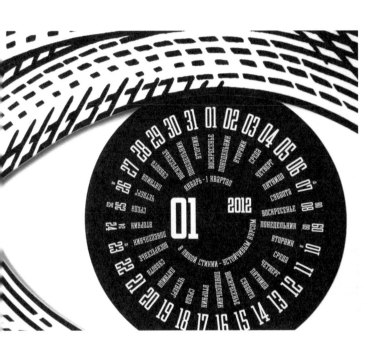

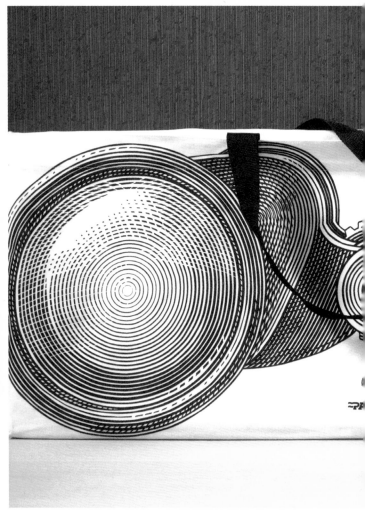

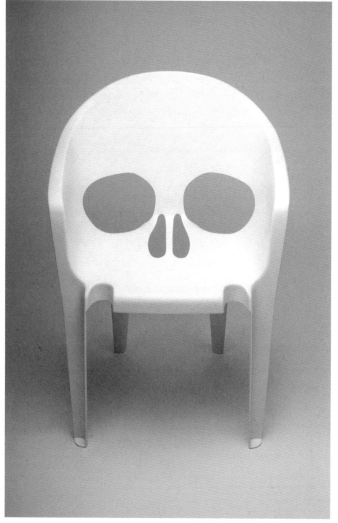

"We wanted to explore new possible expressions and accentuate the main material with carbon fibre in a supporting role, rather than as the star in its own right."

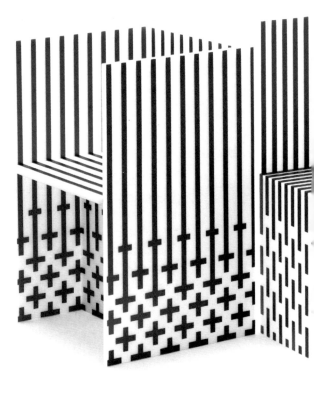

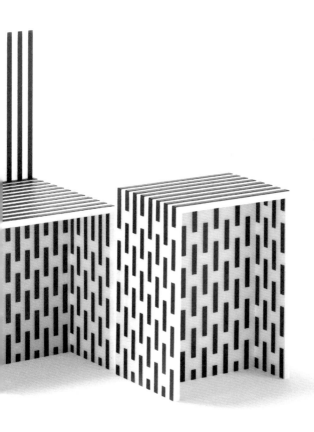

585

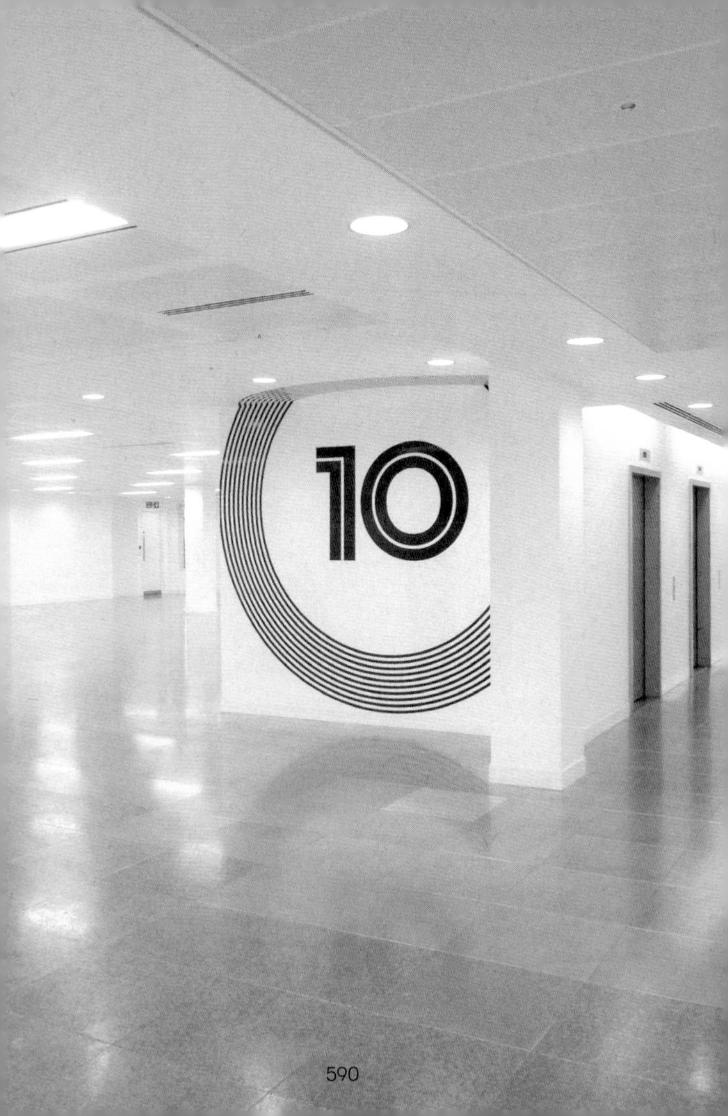
10

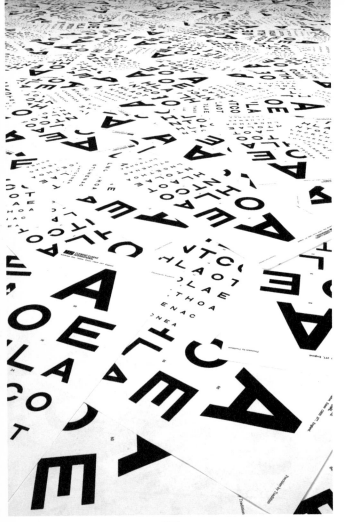

594

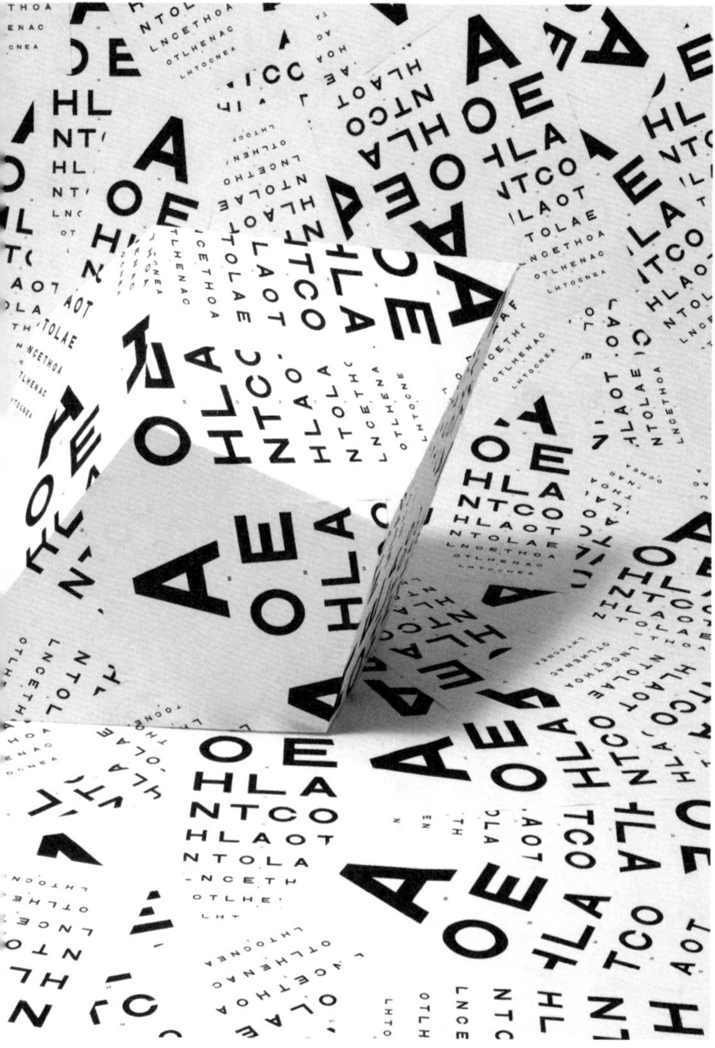

Zeitverwendung Use of time

Für die meisten von uns stellt die Arbeit in einem Beruf das organisierende Zentrum des Lebens dar. Das ist nicht selbstverständlich und war nicht immer so. Aufs ganze Leben gesehen, nimmt die bezahlte Arbeit auch heute nur einen geringen Teil der Zeit ein. Aber sie strahlt auf alle anderen Bereiche ab.

For most of us, work in a particular job makes up the centre around which we organise our lives. That is not automatic, and hasn't always been the case. In terms of our whole lives, paid work still occupies a fairly minor part of our time today, but it does affect all other areas of our lives.

Schlafen
Sleep

Erwerbstätigkeit /
Aus- und Fortbildung

Gainful Employment /
Education and Training

13 %

Unbezahlte Arbeit
Unpaid Work

15 %

34 %

Durchschnittliche tägliche Zeitverwendung von Personen ab 10 Jahren
Average daily use of time by individuals aged 10 and over

Essen / Körperpflege
Eating / Personal Hygiene

12 %

Sport / Hobbys / Spiele /
Mediennutzung

Sports / Hobbies / Games /
Use of Media

17 %

Kontakte /
Veranstaltungen
Contacts / Events

9 %

Unbezahlte Arbeit
Unpaid work

25 h

Bezahlte Arbeit
Paid work

17 h

Frauen
Women

Frauen
Women

Männer
Men

Männer
Men

Arbeitsstunden pro Woche von Personen ab 10 Jahren
Working hours per week by individuals aged 10 and over

Bezahlte und unbezahlte Arbeit

Paid and unpaid work

Arbeit und Freizeit voneinander zu unterscheiden ist gar
nicht so einfach. Was der eine gerne macht und als Erholung
ansieht, tut der andere nur notgedrungen und empfindet
es als Arbeit. Auch die Bezahlung ist kein allzu brauchbares
Kriterium, denn die unbezahlte Arbeitszeit übersteigt die
bezahlte deutlich – zumindest bei Frauen.

It is not always easy to distinguish between work and
leisure. There are some activities that certain people view as
relaxation, which others put down as work. Payment is not
a particularly useful criterion, as unpaid working hours
clearly outweigh paid working hours – at least for women.

599

Arbeitslosigkeit
Unemployment

1 868 504

073 576

459 489

154 523

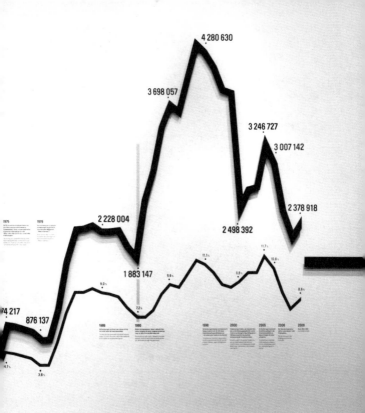

hen Violent crime

International statistics on violent crime used to be taken with a pinch of salt, as every country defines and registers crime differently. Regardless of this, the attempt to record the causes of violence and crime, generally social inequality and pervasive poverty for example, is one of the great challenges before us. One important reason for doing so is work: each resort to aggression and give individuals no feeling they can actually shape their own lives and the crimines they live in.

Trinkwasser Drinking water

Wie für uns selbstverständlich ist. Ist in vielen Regionen der Erde eine Frage um Leben oder Tod: der Zugang zu sauberen Trinkwasser. Experten gehen davon aus, dass im Wassermangel ein wesentlicher Grund für kriegerische Auseinandersetzungen in der Zukunft liegen wird. Der Erhalt, die Herstellung und die Verteilung der Ressource Wasser gehört zu einer der drängendsten Aufgaben.

Something we take for granted in parts of the world is a matter of life and death in other parts: access to clean drinking water. Experts anticipate that water shortages will be a major cause of war and conflict in the years to come. Preserving, producing and distributing water as a resource is one of the most urgent tasks facing us.

g zu Bildung Access to education

Reading and writing skills are key requirements for education,
and thus for the opportunity to reach complete activities and
occupations, in international comparison, there are vast major
differences in the education in deprived/non-available. Nearly
big the instance of knowing the most interesting topic of the
near future.

Lebenserwartung Life expectancy

From a statistical perspective, people are getting older and
older. The reasons we have to remove that more and more
people have the means to survive at the same time. Yet life
expectancy is very varied in around the world. This is mainly
due to differing access to food and medicine, but also many
basic living and working conditions and the risk caused by
exposure to war and violence.

Ar

JR静岡駅北口
葵タワー3階

開館記念展10月より

5〜9月までは講演会や
ワークショップ等を随時開催

開館時間 10:00−19:00 月曜休館
5月1日(土)は12時開館

静岡市美術館
SHIZUOKA CITY
MUSEUM of ART

静岡市美術館
SHIZUOKA CITY
MUSEUM of ART

静岡市美術館
SHIZUOKA CITY
MUSEUM of ART

静岡市美術館
SHIZUOKA CITY
MUSEUM of ART

2010年5月1日〔土〕開館

静岡市美術館 〒420-0852 静岡市葵区紺屋町17-1 葵タワー3F Aoi Tower 3F, 17-1, Kouya-machi, Aoi-ku, Shizuoka, 420-0852 JAPAN tel. 054-273-1515 fax. 054-273-1518 www.shizubi.jp

CAFE +
MUSEU

SHOP

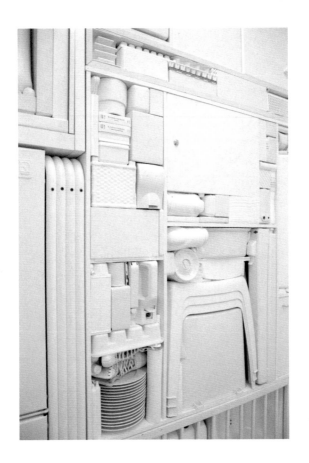

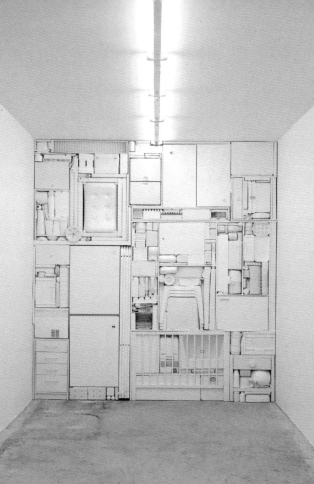

"In a broad sense, all objects within the installation can be described as white, but in context, the gradations towards blue, red or yellow suddenly become clear when seen one by one."

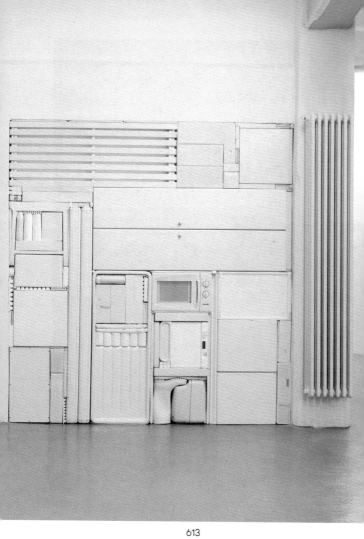

613

INDEX

BIOGRAPHY

10inc.

www.10inc.jp

Founded by award-winning graphic designer and art director Masahiro Kakinokihara in 2007, 10inc. is a Tokyo-based
design studio specialising in branding, graphic design,
advertising, and poster design. It is driven to produce work
that balances concept and craft.

PP. 604–607

Acne JR

www.acnejr.com

A member of the Acne family alongside Acne and Acne Studios,
Acne JR is a Swedish toy brand that aims to create traditional
and iconic toys in a modern way that is also eco-friendly and
inspiring for children. The toys are designed and produced by
Stockholm-based creative studio JR-Work-Shop.

PP. 438–445, 449–453

ART+COM

artcom.de

Building upon the foundation of the design organisation
formed by the Berlin University of Arts, ART+COM officially
became a design studio in 1998 to explore art, science, and
technology in the creation of innovative, unexpected, and
experimental projects.

PP. 598–603

Artiva Design

www.artiva.it

Artiva Design is a multidisciplinary studio in Genoa that specialises in graphic design, branding, and visual communication. Founded in 2003 by Daniele De Batté and Davide Sossi, its projects focus on the presence or absence of graphic elements in geometry and the use of a rigorous grid system that veers naturally towards minimalism.

PP. 037–047, 068–071

Asylum

theasylum.com.sg

Asylum is an award-winning creative company based in Singapore. Since its inception in 1999, it has worked on cross-disciplinary projects that include interactive design, product development, environmental and interior design, packaging, apparel design, as well as branding and graphic design.

PP. 230–235, 496–499

Atelier Christian von der Heide

christianvonderheide.de

Specialising in product, identity, and editorial design, Christian von der Heide has received and been nominated for various awards. Currently based in Hamburg, his clients have included institutions Strellson and 4711, as well as international celebrities such as Dita Von Teese and Michael Michalsky.

PP. 356–359

Atipus

www.atipus.com

Believing in the power of conceptual, creative, and simple designs, Atipus is a Barcelona-based graphic communication studio specialising in corporate identities, art direction, packaging design, as well as editorial and web services. It has won many local and European design honours including ADG-Laus awards and an ADC*E award.

PP. 390–393

Automatico Studio

www.automaticostudio.ch

Founded in 2007, Automatico Studio (formerly known as Demian Conrad Design) applies a methodology of subtraction to the design of visual identities, art books, exhibition catalogues, and products, amongst others. Its philosophy is rooted in 'die gute form' ('the good form') or minimalist art.

PP. 224–226, 228–229

Averill, Brogen

www.brogenaverill.com

An Auckland-based graphic designer who works with an extensive client list and niche design projects, Brogen Averill set up his own studio upon returning from Europe in 2004. Its concept-led work is influenced by European design culture and applied onto a diverse range of mediums.

PP. 448, 549–553

Balmer Hählen

www.balmerhahlen.ch

Founded by Yvo Hählen and Priscilla Balmer, Balmer Hählen was A3 Collectif/Studio before it evolved into its current form in 2017. The award-winning Lausanne-based studio is driven by collaborations and creative explorations with designers, stylists, artists, and photographers. It also specialises in beautiful and high-quality prints.

PP. 072, 084–089

BangBang

bangbang.ca

Founded by Simon Laliberté, BangBang is a Montréal-based creative studio with an integrated approach towards graphic design and screen-printing. Its work centers on the development of distinctive, playful, and strategic concepts that the team skilfully adapts to the reality and needs of each client.

PP. 176–181, 254–263

Barton, John

behance.net/johnbarton

John Barton is a British graphic designer who freelances for well-established UK-based studios. Specialising in graphic design, branding, and typography, he enjoys screen-printing – taking up both commissioned work and independent projects.

PP. 206–211

BERG

BERG was an independent UK-based ideas studio that focused on seamless designs across a wide range of interdisciplinary media including prints, screens, and the environment. It had an international reputation for innovation, imagination, and sound commercial values.

PP. 073–075

BLOW
www.blow.hk

Established in 2010 by Ken Lo who graduated from HKU SPACE Community College in visual communication and won the title of 'Design Student of the Year', BLOW is a Hong Kong-based studio that specialises in visual identities, branding, packaging, print, publications, environmental graphics, and website design.

PP. 242–247, 426–431

Borka, Todd
facebook.com/borkatodd

A French illustrator working in youth literature and magazines, Todd Borka enjoys mixing the aesthetics of Indian ink with the multiplicity of possibilities offered by image editing software.

PP. 416–419

Bossuet, Emmanuel

www.eemstudio.com

Emmanuel Bossuet is a French art director and decorative artist who first entered the industrial design field in the late 1990s. He soon discovered his passion for fashion, creating patterns and prints alongside his product design practice. Today, he works closely with luxury fashion brands worldwide through his studio, EEM.

PP. 532–537

Bravo&Tango

www.bravoandtango.co.uk

Founded by Dan Osman who is an independent creative designer with over 10 years of experience working with well-loved brands from his base in London, Bravo&Tango creates simple, elegant, and memorable design solutions in the form of brand identities, literature, typography, editorial pieces, and web-based media.

PP. 294–299

Bunch

www.bunchdesign.com

A leading London-based design studio specialising in branding, editorial design as well as digital media and motion graphics, Bunch's diverse portfolio includes work with renowned brands like BBC, Nike, Diesel, Sony, Sky, and Red Bull.

PP. 474–483

Bureau Rabensteiner

bureaurabensteiner.at

Bureau Rabensteiner is a branding and graphic design studio based in the heart of the Alps in Innsbruck, Austria. It focuses on strategic thinking and the creation of meaningful designs for clients with varying needs. From branding to packaging, it has built a reputation for crafting high-quality solutions on diverse platforms.

PP. 170–175

C100 Purple Haze

C100 Purple Haze was a Munich-based multidisciplinary design consultancy founded by Christian Hundertmark and Clemens Baldermann. It worked with public and private clients on a variety of national and international projects including conception, art direction, typography, design, and illustration to deliver inventive and precise visual solutions.

P. 020

Campaign

www.campaigndesign.co.uk

Campaign is a London-based award-winning retail design agency that specialises in developing integral brand experiences and design services. The team consists of talents from a diverse range of backgrounds including architecture, film, interior design, graphic design, and product design.

PP. 614–617

Case Studyo

www.casestudyo.com

Launched by Ghent-based creative agency TOYKYO, Case Studyo is a producer and publisher of artwork by contemporary artists. Its dedicated focus lies in creating limited- and open edition objects as well as art with a striking visual language in collaboration with creative talents around the world.

PP. 518–523

Caserne

caserne.com

Caserne's services gravitate around a central point: the client. From consulting to brand strategy and design, the creative team is engaged in maximising the impact and benefits of every touchpoint. The Montréal-based studio is helmed by co-partners and creative directors Ugo Varin Lachapelle and Léo Breton-Allaire.

PP. 410–413

Chen, Hao-En

behance.net/haoenchen

Hao-En Chen is a graphic designer based in Taiwan who is obsessed with creating beautiful things and immersing himself in a fantasy world through his METAMORPHOSIS studio. He is inspired mostly by his own life experiences to discover more creative possibilities.

PP. 102–105

Coco

coco.bzh

French designer and graphic artist Coco applies her background as a communication consultant for leading fashion designers and the founder of her own creative and technology consultancy into her work today. She finds inspiration in a wide variety of places and aims for restraint and minimalism in each project.

PP. 506–511

COMMUNE

commune-inc.jp

Motivated by the will to make things better, COMMUNE sets out to encourage a change in society. Based in Sapporo, the creative team specialises in graphic design and creates work that can take people by surprise, awaken their emotions, and move them to tears.

PP. 402–403

Company

Founded in 2006, Company was a London-based graphic design studio that took a tactile and simple approach to its work — believing that the most successful outcomes contained strong ideas with a playful twist. Besides winning awards, its work was also exhibited nationwide.

PP. 420–425

Dalmau, Alex

alexdalmau.com

Alex Dalmau is a Sydney-based creative who specialises in graphic design, branding, and visual identities. His client list has included Progess, Mandarin Oriental Barcelona, Carolina Herrera, Adidas, Ricola, Font Vella, and Reig Capital.

PP. 236–241, 372–375

Del Valle, Cesar

An arts graduate from the Universidad de Antioquia in Medellin, Cesar Del Valle's work has been exhibited locally and internationally since 2006. He seeks to question the concept of reality and reflect his findings in their truest aesthetic sense.

PP. 538–543

dn&co.

dnco.com

Run by directors Ben Dale and Joy Nazzari, dn&co. is a London-based creative agency that strives to achieve fresh and effective brand, marketing, and communications strategies. It is inspired by culture and place.

PP. 589–591

Dowling, Marie-Niamh

Marie-Niamh Dowling is an independent graphic designer based in Mainz. She graduated in communication design from Hochschule RheinMain in Wiesbaden, and has kept a low profile ever since. Her work has been featured on several online platforms to date.

PP. 227, 350–353

Edited
www.edited.hk

Founded in 2011 by Hong Kong-based graphic designer Renatus Wu, Edited is a design studio that works across a variety of mediums. It specialises in publication, identity, and print design – showcasing a clean and minimalist approach through its thoughtful creative output.

PP. 319–323

Emily Forgot
www.emilyforgot.co.uk

Emily Forgot is the moniker of London-based designer and illustrator Emily Alston. Approaching all briefs with creative thought, originality, humour, and beauty in mind, she develops her own range of products as well as commercial projects for various clients.

PP. 433–437, 485–487, 548

emuni Inc.

www.emuni.co.jp

Design practice emuni Inc. was founded by art directors Takashi and Masashi Murakami in 2012. Based in Tokyo, the studio is involved in a wide range of art direction work, as well as web design, graphic design, branding, book binding, packaging, and product design.

PP. 076–079

Eumann, Jan

Jan Eumann is a creative director at Wolff Olins in Brooklyn with a strong passion for comprehensive brand design and strategic thinking. He strives to develop design systems that bring strategy to life in the most compelling, unexpected, and impactful ways.

PP. 288–293

Feb Design

Founded in 2009, Feb Design was a design collective based in Oporto led by Marta Fragata and Miguel Batista. It specialised in multidisciplinary projects involving corporate identities, branding, wayfinding systems, websites, packaging, and book design.

PP. 248–253

FIBA Design Studio

www.fibadesign.com

A Coimbra-based multidisciplinary creative studio led by
Miguel Batista, FIBA creates brand communication design
systems across digital and traditional media. It specialises
in brand development, print media, web design, as well as
signage systems.

PP. 248–253

filthymedia

www.filthymedia.com

Established in 2004, filthymedia works for in a variety of
fields, including fashion and music. Born in Brighton with a
passion for creating and growing brands, its international
portfolio includes graphic design, art direction, typography,
web/motion design, illustration and photography work.

PP. 150–155, 411

Fons Hickmann m23

fonshickmann.com

Founded in 2001 and run by Bjoern Wolf and Fons Hickmann,
Fons Hickmann m23 is an award-winning Berlin-based
studio that focuses on the design of complex communication systems mainly in the cultural field. It lends its
expertise to everything related to events, communication,
and visual identity.

PP. 190–195

Garrett, Michael

mgarrett.xyz

Michael Garrett is a graphic and web designer based in the US who specialises in visual identities, promotional materials, marketing, creative writing, and socially responsible design practices.

Graphic Design Studio by Yurko Gutsulyak

www.gstudio.com.ua

Yurko Gutsulyak began his design career in 2001 and founded his own Kyiv-based studio in 2005. Besides having his work published and exhibited internationally in countries like France, Poland, and China, he has also won numerous international awards and was elected as the first president of Ukraine's Art Directors Club in 2010

Greece is for Lovers

www.greeceisforlovers.com

Greece is for Lovers is a product design boutique founded by Thanos Karampatsos and Christina Kotsilelou. It sets out to introduce a natural sense of 'Greekness' by promoting Greek culture and design through exquisite products that merge the past and the present.

Hansen, Michael

behance.net/michaelhansen

A visual communication graduate from the School of Design at the Royal Danish Academy of Fine Arts, Michael Hansen is an art director and designer based in Copenhagen who works primarily with conceptual ideas that explore the world of graphic design, fashion photography, and visual identities.

PP. 300–305

Happycentro

happycentro.it

Founded in 1998 in Verona, Happycentro is a design/photo/video workshop that mixes complexity, order, and fatigue to produce beauty. In addition to commissioned work, the team spends plenty of time and energy on researching and testing visual art, typography, graphic design, illustration, animation, film, and music experiments.

PP. 347–349

HelloMe

hellome.studio

A Berlin-based design studio that strives to define contemporary culture, HelloMe focuses on art direction, graphic design, and typography. Using a systematic design approach, it creates and implements innovative communication strategies and distinctive dynamic visual systems.

PP. 164–165

Here Design

www.heredesign.co.uk

Founded by Kate Marlow, Caz Hildebrand, and Mark Paton in 2005, Here Design is a multidisciplinary design collective in London that specialises in design and strategic thinking for branding, packaging, print, publishing, point-of-sale, products, and websites. The studio has won multiple awards locally and internationally.

PP. 279–281

High Tide

hightidenyc.com

High Tide is a full-service creative agency based in New York City that offers brand strategy, identity design, packaging design, production, art direction, campaign development, as well as website design and development services. Founded in 2008, it has since built and helped to grow countless startup companies and legacy brands.

PP. 282–287

iA

ia.net

Founded in Tokyo in 2005 with additional studios in Berlin and Zurich today, iA (formerly Information Architects) offers expert advice on how to position, design, market, and grow digital businesses by connecting the dots. Its client list has included renowned brands like Red Bull, Vogue, Asics, Nikkei, and NHK.

PP. 140–145

Johansson, Michael

www.michaeljohansson.com

Upon completing his studies in Norway and Germany, Michael Johansson returned to Sweden for his master's degree at the Malmö Art Academy. Since then, he has taken part in several residencies and is exhibited frequently both within and outside of Sweden.

Kasper Pyndt Studio

kasperpyndt.dk

Kasper Pyndt is a type- and graphic designer from Copenhagen. The starting point and main engine of his practice is type, language, and the relationship between the two. Through this exchange, he aims to develop straight-forward design solutions that emphasise conceptual sturdiness and contextual (self-)awareness.

Kasper-Florio

kasper-florio.ch

Based in St. Gallen, Larissa Kasper and Rosario Florio are two graphic designers with a strong focus on art direction and typography. Through Kasper-Florio, they collaborate on various projects, mainly using printed matter, in the fields of music and culture.

Kelava, Josip
www.josipkelava.com

Josip Kelava is an award-winning Croatian designer whose connection to the design world correlates with his passion for typography and the thrill of creating something from nothing. With a focus on making his work bold and memorable, he also specialises in brand identity, lettering, photography, and creative direction.

PP. 022–029

Kent, Alexander
www.alexander-kent.com

Alexander Kent is a British photographer who began showing interest in the field from a young age. After growing a career in the fashion industry, he eventually set up his own studio to focus more on still life photography and has not looked back since.

PP. 594–597

Lava
lava.nl

With offices in Amsterdam and Beijing, Lava is an international creative agency with strong roots in editorial design. Working as visual storytellers over the years has led to its unique approach to identity and communication design by its diverse team of graphic, motion, and interactive designers today.

PP. 218–223

Leterme Dowling

Leterme Dowling was a multidisciplinary design studio that worked across different applications and platforms. The founders of Leterme Dowling eventually went on to set up Counterprint, a publishing house and online bookstore based in the UK.

PP. 058–063

Lo Siento

www.losiento.net

Lo Siento is a Barcelona-based studio that specialises in conceptualising for visual identity projects. Its main strength and focus lie in an organic and physical approach to design solutions, resulting in a sweet spot where graphic and industrial design meet and dialogue. The team also enjoys finding ways to work with artisanal processes.

PP. 414–415

Mark Brooks Graphik Design

www.markbrooksgraphikdesign.com

Currently working as a brand director at Behance and creative director for 99U, Mark Brooks specialises in art direction, graphic design, illustration, typography, and branding. He has participated in various design conferences, exhibits, and lectures worldwide.

P. 021

Martiszu

martiszu.com

Marta Ludwiszewska a.k.a. Martiszu is a freelance graphic designer and illustrator living and working in Warsaw. Her work focuses on typography and illustration on print. Besides being the co-founder of screen-printing studio N22, she also plays a big part in Full Moon Party, an independent artistic initiative to promote Polish urban art.

PP. 132–139

Metcalf, Jordan

jordan-metcalf.com

Based in Portland, Jordan Metcalf is a South Afrian designer who focuses on diverse, experimental custom lettering and identity design. An ADC Young Gun winner in 2013, he loves typography, illustration, good design, and a combination of all three. Jordan has also been involved in murals, exhibitions, and speaking engagements.

PP. 570–571

Murmure

murmure.me

Based in Caen and Paris, Murmure is a French creative communications agency specialising in strong visual identities. Led by Julien Alirol Ressencourt and Paul, it focuses on singular creative projects with aesthetics adapted to its clients' aims and objectives.

PP. 030–035, 118–129, 360–365, 484

nendo

nendo.jp

Founded in 2002 by architect Oki Sato, Tokyo-based nendo strives to bring small surprises to people through various multidisciplinary practices and media touchpoints such as architecture, interiors, furniture, industrial products, and graphic design. It aims to reshape the everyday through intuitive and interesting experiences.

PP. 580–587

Neubau

neubauberlin.com

Defined by a systematic approach to type as well as print, screen, and space design, Berlin-based Neubau was founded by Stefan Gandl in 2001. Besides releasing bestselling books like 'Neubau Welt' (2005), 'Neubau Modul' (2007), and 'Neubau Forst Catalogue' (2014), Stefan has also had his works internationally exhibited and published.

PP. 554–563

Nieminen, Lotta

www.lottanieminen.com

Lotta Nieminen is a multidisciplinary Finnish designer and illustrator who set up her eponymous graphic design, art direction, and illustration studio in New York. She is passionate about finding the best tools to execute content-driven visuals by working as a creative partner in bringing thoughtfully crafted visual identities to life.

PP. 264–271

NOMO Design

shop.nomodesign.com

A multidisciplinary creative studio based in Chicago, NOMO was founded in 2010 by architect and designer Jerome Daksiewicz. Through intent listening, research, and questioning, the studio works closely with clients to craft meaningful, strategic, and integrated design solutions.

PP. 113–117

---

nomo®creative

nomocreative.com

Founded in 2015 by professionals from various backgrounds, nomo®creative is a design studio based in Taiwan. Driven by concise and contemporary design with a distinct touch, it explores every inch of the creative process and seeks to engage with cultures and humanity

PP. 096–101, 312–317

Non-Format

non-format.com

Founded by Kjell Ekhorn and Jon Forss, Non-Format believes in the importance of bespoke design solutions. From its office bases in the Twin Cities, USA, and Oslo, Norway, the design studio's approach focuses on expressive imagery and custom typography to balance each client's desire to connect with customers on an emotional level.

PP. 130–131

Not Available

behance.net/notavailable

Not Available is a multidisciplinary studio in Hong Kong that specialises in design strategies, art direction, interactive media, as well as space design. It believes that design is not a 'solo game' and that every party plays an important role in the creative process to accomplish great work.

PP. 404–409

0.00 Design & Risograph ROOM

odotoo.com

0.00 is a Taipei-based design studio that combines risograph printing technology with experimental design patterns. Founded by two graphic designers, it specialises in fusing creative printing methods with product development.

PP. 090–095

POOL

poolhouse.eu

Founded by Léa Padovani and Sébastien Kieffer in 2010, POOL is a Paris-based creative studio that takes design beyond furniture, graphics, artistic direction, and interior architecture. Based on 'outside the box' thinking, its work features off-beat, dreamlike, and at times melancholic qualities, while always remaining functional.

PP. 572–573

Poulain, Damien

damienpoulain.com

Damien Poulain is a graphic artist and designer who splits his time between London and Paris. He is involved in a wide range of art, fashion, and music projects – gaining international recognition for his commercial and artistic work along the way.

Poulsen, Mads Jakob

madsjakobpoulsen.com

Recognised by the likes of Print Magazine, D&AD, iF Design Awards, and the Creative Circle Awards, Mads Jakob Pouslen is a Danish designer who has been amongst the top 50 designers of the world as chosen by Art Directors Club New York. He is also the founder of Poulsen Projects, his eponymous independent studio.

Raffinerie AG für Gestaltung

raffinerie.com

Established in 2000, Raffinerie AG is an award-winning creative studio based in Zurich that specialises in design solutions that last. Through its talented team of graphic artists and illustrators, it takes a holistic approach in each of its projects to meet its clients' needs.

République Studio

www.republique.studio

République Studio is an award-winning creative direction and graphic design practice based in Paris. The team works with local and international clients across a diverse range of platforms and disciplines, using typography as one of the key elements of its work. Its strength lies in its versatile and modern design, often inspired by the zeitgeist.

PP. 166–169

Ribeiro, Rui

Rui Ribeiro is a graphic designer who worked mostly on print and typography. After completing his studies in Portugal and the UK, he was attached to Hyperakt in New York for clients on cultural and social change, as well as COLORS Magazine in Italy.

PP. 184–189, 216

Riera, Maximo

maximoriera.com

Based in Cadiz, Maximo Riera has been a practicing artist for over 30 years. Besides predominantly working in photography, painting, and sculpture, he has also published a collection of poetry and organised several exhibitions with all proceeds going to charity.

PP. 574–579

Root

www.thisisroot.co.uk

Based in London, Root is a full-service independent creative studio that was founded by Martin Root in 1990. Driven by design, it strives to deliver innovative and effective solutions for a diverse pool of clients all over the world. Its range of services span grapic design, art direction, advertising, and motion pictures.

PP. 278, 354–355

Ruddigkeit, Raban / + Ruddigkeit

ruddigkeit.de

Raban Ruddigkeit is a designer, editor, and illustrator in Berlin who founded his own agency after 20 years in the advertising and graphic design industry. His focus lies in uniting great ideas and great execution with analogue and digital technologies. He has won more than 150 international awards to date.

PP. 182–183

ruiz+company

www.ruizcompany.com

Led by David Ruiz, ruiz+company specialises in creating innovative brand concepts, codes, corporate identities, advertising, packaging, and broadcast design solutions. Based in Barcelona, the studio has been honoured with more than 100 local and international awards, on top of being featured by notable publications worldwide.

PP. 080–083

Sitoh inc.

www.sitoh.co.jp

Sitoh inc. seeks to bring individuals, cultures, and societies together through the power of design. Established in 2016 by Motoi Shito, the studio produces dynamic and effective graphics that communicate its ideas – culminating in a diverse design portfolio.

PP. 052–057

Smel

www.smel.net

Founded in 2001 by Edgar Smaling and Carlo Elias, Smel is a design agency in Amsterdam that consists of a dynamic team of dedicated and multidisciplinary creatives. It specialises in strategic corporate identities, magazines, books, websites, as well as illustrious design concepts that subtly unite quality and imagination.

PP. 106–111, 156–161

Studio Astrid Stavro

www.astridstavro.com

Astrid Stavro Studio is an independent design consultancy that was founded in Barcelona in 2004 and currently based in Majorca. It is renowned internationally for its discerning editorial design with a strong emphasis on clean, distinctive, and considered typography.

PP. 202–205

Studio Feixen

www.studiofeixen.ch

Formerly known as FEIXEN: Design by Felix Pfäffli, Studio Feixen is an independent design studio based in Lucerne. It creates visual concepts that focus specifically on nothing in particular. Whether it is graphic design, interior design, fashion design, type design or animation, the team is interested in projects that challenges it.

PP. 500–501

Studio Marcus Kraft

www.marcuskraft.net

An award-winning graphic design office based in Zurich, Studio Marcus Kraft works on diversified disciplines including art direction, graphic design, conceptualisation, and typography with an emphasis on creativity and quality. It creates custom-made projects for local and international clients.

PP. 592–593

STUDIO NEWWORK

studionewwork.com

A branding and creative studio based in New York, STUDIO NEWWORK assembles passionate typographic designers with a commitment to excellence in design. Besides working across a range of media spanning print, screen graphics, products, and environmental designs, it has also published a large-format arts publication, NEWWORK MAGAZINE.

PP. 212–215

STUDIOLAV

www.studiolav.com

STUDIOLAV is a London-based design studio that thrives on reinterpreting ideas with a playful and ironic twist by investigating tendencies and curiosities regarding perceptions of form and materiality. Besides its own product line, the team also works on interior design projects for a variety of clients.

PP. 376–381

Talmor, Morey / Talmor & Talmor & Talmor

andtalmor.com

Talmor & Talmor & Talmor is an award-winning New York-based creative consultancy and design agency founded by Morey Talmor. It focuses on creating work that spans multiple disciplines including branding, creative direction, design for digital platforms, editorial, packaging, as well as content creation.

PP. 524–527

The Hello Poster Show

hellopostershow.com

Founded by Benjamin K. Shown and Alanna MacGowan in 2009, The Hello Poster Show based in Seattle is an outlet for designers to flex creative muscles for a good cause. Each collection is based on different themes and colour palettes, with proceeds from sales donated to benefit local charities.

PP. 488–495

This Studio

www.this-studio.co.uk

Founded by David Bennett in 2005, This Studio is a UK-based design studio that produces creative work with a focus on graphic design, branding, and poster designs with a strong typographic style. David is also the founder of Visuelle, an online design showcase website.

PP. 010–019

Toby Ng Design

www.toby-ng.com

Prior to starting his own design firm in Hong Kong in 2014, Toby Ng spent years honing his craft in London and Singapore — picking up several awards along the way. He rigorously tackles design challenges with wit and aesthetically meaningful communication methodologies.

PP. 272–277, 336–345, 366–371

Tokyo-Go-Go Illustration Studio

Tokyo-Go-Go Illustration Studio was a project by Durban-based designer, illustrator, and animator Greg Darroll that combined his studio skills with his freelance experiences. He is renowned for an illustration style that showcases a strong sense of personality with the perfect amount of detail.

PP. 528–531

TOYKYO

www.toykyo.be

Founded in 2006 by Mathieu Van Damme and Benjamin Van Oost, TOYKYO aims to spread happiness by producing beautiful objects and refreshing designs with a dash of fun. The Belgium-based creative agency consists of a diverse team specialising in design, product development, and advertising.

PP. 460–471

Vayreda, Francesc Moret

francescmoret.com

Francesc Moret Vayreda appreciates timelessness and the simplicity of design. His eponymous graphic design studio in Barcelona specialises in corporate identities and branding work, based on the underlying approach that each design should narrate a concept and stand for more than just its visual form.

PP. 382–385

Walker, Stewart

Stewart Walker graduated from the Duncan of Jordanston Art and Design College in Dundee. Currently based in London, the graphic deisgner specialises in typography, branding, and book design.

PP. 472–473

Wang, Zhi Hong

wangzhihong.com

Zhi Hong Wang is one of the most iconic graphic designers in Taipei and has been a member of AGI since 2015. Under his own studio, he has been recognised by various international design organisations since 2000.

Wudai Shiguo

Wudai Shiguo or WDSG was a Hong Kong-based branding and advertising creative boutique set up by iconic local designer Kenji Wong. It set out to provide revolutionary concepts through reformation while respecting the classics and timeless craftsmanship.

Acknowledgements

We would like to specially thank all the designers and studios who are featured in this book for their significant contribution towards its compilation. We would also like to express our deepest gratitude to our producers for their invaluable advice and assistance throughout this project, as well as the many professionals in the creative industry who were generous with their insights, feedback, and time. To those whose input was not specifically credited or mentioned here, we truly appreciate your support.

Future Editions

If you wish to participate in viction:ary's future projects and publications, please send your portfolio to:
submit@victionary.com